DATE			

YAIR KOTLER

HEIL KAHANE

YAIR KOTLER

HEIL KAHANE

Adama Books, New York

Translated by Edward Levin

Copyright © 1986

Computerized typography, including automatic pagination,
by M. Rachlin Printing

Library of Congress Cataloging-in-Publication Data
Kotler, Yair.
Heil Kahane
1. Kahane,   Meir.   2.   Israel.   Knesset   –   Biography.
3. Rabbis – United States – Biography. 4. Revisionist Zionists –
Biography. 5. Israel – Politics and government. I. Title.

DS126.6.K2K67   1986   956.94'054'0924 [B]   86-1035
ISBN 0-915361-35-3

Printed in the United States of America.

Contents

Introduction

Meir Kahane, member of Knesset, leader of the Kach movement in Israel and one of the founders of the Jewish Defense League in the United States, gave a surprising, if not strange, reason for refusing to grant me an interview when I was doing research for this book: "I'm not interested in being interviewed. You're writing a book about me. I don't want to be interviewed for your book. Some time I'll write a book about myself."

I asked him why he doesn't refuse to be interviewed in the press. He had even filed an appeal with the Israeli High Court of Justice to issue an order compelling the government Israel Broadcast Authority (radio and television) to interview him, and to treat him as the electronic media treat other members of Knesset. He wanted the court to order radio and television to drop the ban they had placed on him. Kahane replied that "It is correct that I am interviewed a lot in the newspapers, even by those who criticize me. I don't care what they write about me as long as they spell my name right. This is accepted in America. Today they read, and tomorrow they forget. But a book is something else, this is for the bookshelf. I'm not interested in a book now. I don't want [this]."

This short conversation took place on September 30, 1984, sixty-seven days after Meir Kahane had been elected to the Eleventh Knesset. I made my request when Kahane was a guest

7

speaker in the Sephardi synagogue "Ben Porat" in Yad Eliyahu, a neighborhood in the southeastern part of Tel Aviv.

Kahane's wild attack on Arabs, bordering on extreme racism, aroused the enthusiasm of the worshippers, who sat on the edge of their chairs, intent on hearing each word of his, and who enthusiastically applauded him.

I wasn't satisfied with Kahane's reply. While I was writing the Hebrew edition of the book, I sent a registered letter to the Jerusalem home of the new member of Knesset, on February 27, 1985. I wrote to Kahane as follows: "On September 30, 1984, in a short conversation with you before your speech in the Sephardi synagogue "Ben Porat" in Yad Eliyahu in Tel Aviv, I asked you to designate a meeting with me, for the purpose of receiving answers from you to the questions which I wanted to ask you in the course of writing a book about you, but, unfortunately, I did not receive an affirmative reply. Once again I turn to you with the same request. I would be very grateful if you would set a date for holding the interview."

Two months passed. The mailman returned the letter to me, with the stamp "Not Requested." Kahane refused to accept the registered letter, which bore my name and address on the back.

In the course of writing this book, I spoke with and interviewed more than 100 people in Israel and the United States, including the founders of the Jewish Defense League in both countries, and the heads of the Kach movement. The long conversation I had in New York with Shlomo M. Russ (Raziel) was extremely productive. The young sociologist-psychologist had spent years preparing his doctoral thesis "The Zionist Hooligans," on the actions of the Jewish Defense League and the manner in which it was run. The information I received from Russ completely matched the results of my own research. Reading Russ's thesis aided me in my research, and saved me much precious time.

I also obtained much valuable information from Alan M. Dershowitz's book *The Best Defense*. The chapter "The Borough Park Connection" told the dramatic story of the traitor within the ranks of the JDL, who revealed to Dershowitz, one of the most brilliant lawyers in the United States, the motives which led him to serve the authorities as an informer, while within the top echelon of the League, turning over to the police his closest friends and those who trusted him.

The book was originally written and published in Hebrew. In the course of translating the book, various changes have been made, including condensing much of the original text. New chapters have also been added. Many events have occurred in Israel since the writing of the Hebrew text, including the racist outburst against Arabs in the city of Afula, which was unprecedented in its intensity in Arab-Jewish relations in Israel, and whose fruits were reaped by Meir Kahane.

At the end of 1985, Meir Kahane was the best-known Jewish racist throughout the world, harming Israel's democratic image and unbalancing the delicate fabric of the relationship which has developed between Jews and Arabs since the beginning of the Zionist movement and the Return to Zion of the Jewish people after 2,000 years.

Meir Kahane, the subject of this biography, is truly the Ugly Israeli.

Yair Kotler, Tel Aviv

1

Incitement in Afula

Afula. A sleepy Israeli city in the center of the Jezreel Valley. The founding fathers of the city envisaged it as the "capital of the Valley," but it did not meet this challenge. It was, and remains, a forgotten settlement of around 20,000 people, most of whom came, or are the children of those who came in the waves of mass immigration following the establishment of the State of Israel. Many of the city's inhabitants are Oriental (Sephardic) Jews. Many Arabs, both from Israel proper and from the territories, come to the city to work in those areas of employment which the local Jewish unemployed sneer at. Arabs, not Jews, are employed in garages, *falafel* stands, stores, and the marketplace.

Afula was in an uproar at the end of July 1985, suddenly roused from its summer slumber. The city's weather and politics were both boiling: a pair of teachers, 35-year-old Yossi Eliyahu and 19-year-old Leah Almakais were found murdered in Gilboa, not far from the Arab city of Jenin in the territories. Three young Arabs were quickly apprehended and admitted committing the murder: shepherds from the small village of Arrabuna, in the Jenin district.

Meir Kahane was quick to take advantage of the situation. He appeared in Afula for a quick visit, but was afraid to get out of the car which had brought him to the city. His appearance was enough to heat up the atmosphere and incite the curly-haired young people on the street corners, who see each Arab as a potential threat to their social standing.

Those on the street corners shouted "Kahane the savior!" They attacked Arabs, both from within Israel and the territories who came to Afula to work. They threw stones at Arab cars. "We'll teach you such a lesson, you won't be able to set foot in Afula." They attacked Arabs in the marketplace, and overturned *falafel* stands. They crowded together on the main road and damaged cars bearing license plates from the territories. Kahane's followers led the chorus: "The Arabs must be driven out of Afula, out of the entire country."

When the Arabs stayed away from the city for a few days, their jobs remained vacant. The *falafel* stands, stalls in the marketplace, and the garages were closed. The street corner youth kept killing time and acting wildly. They continued to sit and drink beer. They looted shops. The mob continued to shout "Kahane, Kahane – death to the Arabs," sweeping before it everyone it encountered.

Kahane was not permitted to enter the city. He was warned by the police, but his presence was not necessary. His followers did his dirty work. Kahane achieved his goal: his name was on page one of all the newspapers. His distorted face was seen by millions of viewers in Israel and throughout the world as he shouted, "The only answer is to throw the Arabs out. I want the Arabs out, out, out!"

The city was a volcano. Kahane had set the tone from afar, and fear and hatred were rampant. Passions ran high. The Arab was the enemy.

The police took a strong stand, and prevented a pogrom. They also rescued journalists and cameramen, who had become the scapegoats for Kahane's hooligans, and the target on which to release all their frustrations at seeing the hard-working Arabs attain better economic standing than those Jews who spent their days idly sitting on street corners. They shouted at the newsmen, "You're the servants of the PLO and the terrorists. All the reporters are Communists.... They should all be hanged."

They had learned Kahane's teachings well, and recited them chapter and verse. Even the Likud Deputy Speaker of the Knesset Meir Cohen-Avidov, a racist in his own right (after an Arab terrorist outrage, he had demanded to "crush their innards, tear out their eyes") couldn't steal the show from Kahane. The racists of Afula gave him a warm welcome, and cheered him when he called for death to terrorists, but the mob didn't stop chanting "Kahane, Kahane" (who remained far away, safe in Jerusalem).

Ovadiah Eli, the Likud mayor of Afula, managed to quiet the city after a few days. He maintained his composure and sanity. He refused to be drawn into provocations. He calmed the city and refused Kahane permission to appear in the city square.

Afula during the summer of 1985 was not the same city it once had been. Meir Kahane, the racist who had come to Israel from the United States, had lit a fire.

2

Defender of Jewish Womanhood

Tel Aviv, October 28, 1984 – three months after the Knesset elections. Kahane arrives to hold a press conference, surrounded by a protective circle of his followers. The whole entourage appears wearing black T-shirts, with a circular inscription proclaiming that they are members of the "Jewish Honor Guard." Inside the circle, the Kach symbol, a clenched fist.

Kahane sits at the head of the table. Four muscular men, and one thin, frightened girl stand behind him, arms crossed behind their backs in a military pose. A few more muscular bodyguards stand by the entrance to the hall.

Kahane blinks and begins talking in broken Hebrew. It's difficult to understand him because of his heavy stutter. "We've come here today in order to present before you a problem to be solved. As you know, we were supposed to go to Taibe [an Arab village to the east of Kfar Saba] two weeks ago, to raise there the acute, painful problem of Jewesses married to Arabs. The Minister of Police said that he wasn't willing to permit us to go there, so we appealed to the High Court of Justice. I hope and assume and expect that at least I'll be successful in getting from the High Court the right to go to Taibe as a member of Knesset, and that they'll agree that just as a non-Jewish body has the right to come to Dizengoff [the cafe district of Tel Aviv], so does Kach have the same right to come to Taibe, which is still within the boundaries of the Jewish state."

Kahane mentions the concern of Jewish leaders over inter-marriage and assimilation in the Diaspora, and wonders why this same concern doesn't exist for "this cancer" in Israel, "Jewesses in Israel marrying and going out with Arabs. Once there was a Chief Education Officer in the IDF,* whose role was to educate the IDF – Morele Baron. His daughter married an Arab. OK. He's not to blame, but what was his response? They received the wife and her husband with honor, with no reservations. If this is so, then there's no reason for a Jewish state [he raises his voice for emphasis]. I don't care at all if the press in Israel will label me as a Nazi and a fascist.... The picture of the Jewess in Taibe, the in-laws, and the children. This is a tragedy....

"We're going to wage war on this *cancer*. Before you are some members of the Jewish Honor Guard. These people will be in every city, town, neighborhood, every evening, in patrols, in order to put an end to the phenomenon of Arabs coming from Jenin, Tul Karem, Sahnin, the Shapira quarter in Tel Aviv. An Arab won't go out here with a Jewess. They'll try to explain to him as gently as possible that, thank God, there are beautiful, good, Arab girls in the [Arab] villages. We've stuck up 10,000 of these. [The journalists receive yellow stickers with the Kach symbol and slogan "Never Again" and the inscription, in Hebrew and Arabic, "Arab! Don't dare to even think about a Jewess!"]

"We'll go to her home. We'll try to persuade her that she comes from the glorious Jewish people, and if not – we'll stick up her picture throughout the whole neighborhood: 'This is the traitor to the Jewish People.' I've brought here a Jewess, who's married to an Arab, and who lives in an Arab village. She'll explain to you what it's like to be a Jewess in an Arab village."

Kahane explains that the Israeli "PLO television" didn't cover the conference, and appeals to the journalists present "as a Jew to Jews. Today you aren't journalists. Bring this message to the entire nation."

When asked about Jewish men going out with Arab women,

* Israel Defense Forces

14

Kahane replies by citing the Biblical example of Phineas, who killed a Jew and Midianite woman who had sexual relations. He claims, "I'm not Phineas, since I'm quite moderate.... When the Knesset will raise this odd law against racism, I'll have to cite a lot from the [Jewish] sources, and they'll take the Bible out of the high schools."

A young woman, the subject of the press conference, enters the room. Dark-skinned, somewhat frightened, wearing a blouse and tight white pants, she sits next to Kahane, who presents her as "a Jewess with courage." The bodyguards make threatening noises to the photographers: "She's still got children in that village. She and her children are in danger. No pictures."

Kahane lowers his head towards her: "Talk already."

The young woman, frightened: "What should I say?"

Kahane: "Say something already. Go ahead and talk."

She says she's been married to an Arab for six years, and that she's been trying to get a divorce since the first year they were married.

Avner Uzan, one of Kahane's entourage, whom the girl named responsible for bringing her to Kach: "We try to help girls in trouble, who are under the influence of drugs in Arab villages. A plague that's spreading. The people don't know. They think that everything's fine. Our girls assimilate among the goyim. An Arab changes his name to Yossi. He's handsome and nice, and he's got a Magen David around his neck. After she's fallen in love with him, he says, 'I'm an Arab.'"

The young woman relates that she met her husband on the beach in Haifa. "I knew that he was an Arab [contradicting Uzan's claim – Y. K.]. We fell in love. He told me he was an Arab. I married because I loved him. I've suffered enough blows. He humiliated me. He starved me and my children, and tried to turn me into a prostitute. I went to the police, and they didn't say anything. He was a pimp once and he had a prostitute. I was a slave, not a wife." She told that her in-laws and the neighbors treated her nicely but not her husband. She fled from him with her daughter to a shelter for battered women. Her husband kidnapped the child, and hasn't let her see the girl since. "I don't want to live with an Arab.... I converted to Islam, but returned to Judaism eight months ago."

Kahane is asked if there aren't Jewish husbands who beat their wives. Kahane, showing signs of increasing irritation: "Certainly there are Jews as well as Arabs who beat [their wives], but there is a tremendous difference between the rape of a Jew and an Arab raping Jewesses. The Arab screws both the woman and the state, and that's that. This is why we came here with the woman. She's afraid."

A reporter asks the girl why she didn't run away from her husband. Kahane doesn't give her a chance to answer: "Do you know what it's like there? There's fear and terror there. It's not easy to be a hero there. She isn't afraid any longer, because we're with her. We'll protect her and the rest, who we expect and hope will come to us, in Kach's usual ways. I won't go into the details. We hope to take the children out by the court, or by other means."

Uzan tells of taking the woman to the village at one a.m. to see her children, where her husband received them with stones and broken bottles. "Fifty people from the village assembled. It was a miracle that we could leave. He wanted to keep her. Jewish girls go with Arabs and there's no one to save them."

Kahane is asked whether Kach acts within the law. "I don't care about the law. I care that here there's a mother of Jewish children…. An Arab won't walk around in our neighborhoods. We'll take out women and children by any means at all. Until now we were quite flexible and moderate, since I'm naturally this way, but it won't be this way; if we have to use unacceptable methods, we will. We didn't immigrate to Israel so that a woman like this from Morocco will go out with an Arab, in, of all places, the Holy Land of Ben Gurion and Begin. Her father didn't dream of such a thing…. I'm willing to sit [in jail] for this. We'll propose a law in the Knesset. It won't pass. Except for me and Tawfiq Toubi [from the (Communist) Democratic Front for Peace and Equality party], no one will vote for it. This Guard (he points to his bodyguards) is very serious."

Kahane promises that if the police won't do their work, "we will." Using force? "And how."

An elderly journalist, sporting a French goatee, shouts that

16

the Nazis used similar methods; isn't Kahane afraid of such comparisons?

"Rape is detestable, but I've already mentioned the motives of the Arab rapist. The motive of the Arab and the pimp, like the black who rapes a white woman, is that he knows that he's got power and control over the Jewish state."

Uzan completes the picture: "Let's try to go into an Arab village and try to start with Arab women. How will we emerge from there? The Arabs are taking control of the country.... This could happen to any one of us. They study with us in the universities. They ride with us on the buses. My wife is entitled to ride free on buses because I'm a Dan [bus cooperative] driver, but she doesn't ride on buses. An Arab sits next to her and puts his head on her shoulder. He pretends to fall asleep. I'm losing money because my wife doesn't ride on buses. Let's see one of us ride on an Arab bus. He won't come out alive.... They're spreading out over the whole country, and they're also taking our daughters."

The young woman claims her husband tried to give her drugs; Kahane maintains that there are more than a thousand Jewesses living with Arabs, and that he's enlisted 121 people for the Honor Guard.

Uzan: "Our movement becomes stronger after every [terrorist] attack; too bad only after attacks.... The solution is separation between Jews and Arabs. Our people aren't armed."

I talked with one of Kahane's bodyguards after the press conference. Pima Lifmanovich said that he had been a Prisoner of Zion in Siberia for ten years, from 1940 to 1950. He immigrated to Israel in 1971. He's married with one daughter. He said he was the coach of the Israel under-18 national boxing team. He wanted me to quote him: "Why did they make the state, for the Arabs? Every day Jews flee from the Arabs. A catastrophe. Europe wasn't enough? It wasn't a school? There isn't any police in Israel. They only want salaries.... I came to Israel to help the national state. An Arab who kills a Jew should go to the cemetery, not to prison. Afterwards they grab a Jew in Lebanon and exchange him for a million Arabs."

3

Kahane: Early Years

Who is Meir Kahane? Kahane has never revealed his complete past. He tells the press what he wants it to know, but never answers embarrassing questions. He chooses the participants in his press conferences. When he doesn't like questions he responds with shouts and curses. Whoever asks him provocative questions is the enemy in his eyes.

Meir Kahane was born into a distinguished line of rabbis. Baruch David Kahane, Meir's great-grandfather, was a rabbi in Galicia, then part of the Austro-Hungarian Empire. He immigrated to Palestine in 1850, together with his seven-year-old son, Nahman. Their immigration came in the wake of the call to immigrate to the Holy Land issued by Israel Meir ha-Kohen, better known as the Hafetz Hayim, after his famous book which described the personal qualities a person should strive to attain. Baruch David was the founder of the Khanz Hassidic community in Safed. During World War I, the family was deported to Austria. Nahman discovered that his son Ezekiel Shraga showed great promise as a scholar, and sent him at the age of twelve to Europe to further his religious training. Ezekiel Shraga studied in the Talmudical academies of Auschwitz and Pressburg, in what was then Hungary. He was ordained at the age of 18, in 1924, the same year that he immigrated to the United States. He continued his studies, receiving a doctorate in sociology from Yeshiva University. He served as a pulpit rabbi, and eventually was appointed head of the Flatbush Board of Rabbis. His wife Sonia, unlike her husband, was a difficult, uneducated woman. Their neighbors called her a "witch." He and his wife moved to Israel after retiring, and he died in Jerusalem in 1978. In Meir's opinion, his father had not been properly appreciated by the Jewish community in Flatbush.

Meir was born in Brooklyn as Martin David Kahane on August 1, 1932. His brother Nahman was born five years later, in 1937. The family lived in a modest second-story apartment in Flatbush, a neighborhood in Brooklyn with a large Jewish population. The brothers grew up in a traditional Jewish atmosphere. Their father headed the Revisionist Zionist movement (which in Israel evolved into the Herut Party) in the United States before the establishment of the State of Israel. The leader of the Revisionist movement, Ze'ev Jabotinsky, and other Revisionist leaders visited the Kahane home. Meir met Jabotinsky when he was five years old. During the postwar years, when the Jewish community in Palestine struggled for independence from the British Mandatory authorities, Meir's father raised funds for arms for the Revisionist military organization in Palestine, the Irgun Zvai Leumi.

Martin David was an exceptional child. He was extremely sensitive and emotional to the point of tears. He had to undergo a minor operation at the age of five. The nurse who cared for him was amazed by the child's requesting the *New York Times*. Visitors to the Kahane home reported that they saw the ten-year-old Martin David reading the entry on Karl Marx in the *Encyclopaedia Brittanica*.

Martin David was the captain of his high school's debating team, and was active in sports: he played baseball and basketball, and was on the school's track team, excelling in the 10,000-meter run. He was a fan of the Yankees. In 1957, at the age of 25, two years after marrying, he was ordained as a rabbi by the Mir Yeshivah, one of the leading Talmudic academies in the United States. Now he called himself Meir, and not Martin David. He also studied at Brooklyn College, and received an MA in International Law and International Relations. He received an LLB degree from the New York Law School, but did not pass the New York State bar examinations. People who knew him then said that a good memory was sufficient to become ordained, but passing the bar examinations required the ability to see the other side of the argument, which Kahane never possessed.

Kahane's first experience with the non-Jewish world was in his native Flatbush, which at the time was populated mainly by non-Jews. His first taste of "anti-Semitism" wasn't very serious. The neighborhood bullies delighted in knocking his skullcap to the ground. Kahane didn't let this go unanswered, and ambushed his would-be assailants on street corners. These fights didn't last long, and the "enemies" made their peace by drinking beer together. Kahane later stated that he had a pleasant childhood, with no traumatic experiences. His brother Nahman, who didn't fight back as did Meir, wasn't so fortunate. Once, returning late at night from yeshivah, he was attacked on the subway by four assailants and stabbed behind the ear.

In 1952, when Meir was twenty years old, vandals smeared drawings of swastikas on several synagogues in Brooklyn, close to the Kahane home. Kahane's father protested to the city authorities, but to no avail. In a conversation with his family, the elder Kahane, very depressed, blurted out that it would be a good idea if Jews would organize an underground to defend themselves. The father later recalled that Meir took this seriously, and told his father that this was the only course of action that they could take.

Meir first learned of the Holocaust in 1942, when he was ten. The horrible stories of the destruction of European Jewry were to accompany him for many years. In 1946 he joined Betar, the Revisionist youth movement. He was arrested for the first time a year later, in 1947. Ernest Bevin, the British Foreign Minister who was identified as the architect of Great Britain's anti-Zionist policy in Palestine, came to New York to deliver an address to the United Nations General Assembly. This was at the height of the struggle to establish a Jewish state, and the seizure of "illegal" Jewish immigrants to Palestine and their deportation to Cyprus, or even back to Europe, in the case of the famous shipload of "illegals" on the *Exodus 1947*. Kahane and his comrades from Betar waited at the dock, and pelted Bevin's car with tomatoes and rocks. Kahane was cracked on the skull by a policeman and arrested. His father shouted at him in the police station, blasting him for his behavior. Meir replied that this was his father's responsibility, because he had taught him all this. His father, shocked by his son's reaction, learned his lesson. He never raised his voice to his rebellious son again.

His uncle, Rabbi Isaac Trainin, the head of the religious affairs department of the New York Federation of Jewish Philanthropies, would later state in 1984, after Kahane's election to the Knesset, that he had been an "intriguer" from his youth. This aspect of his personality came to the fore in his career in Betar. Despite his charismatic personality, and the fact that he was popular with girls, his arrogance antagonized many leaders in Betar, who thought that he was too immature to fulfill his ambitions of quickly filling a key leadership position in the youth movement. In 1951, at the age of 19, Kahane was turned down when he requested to be appointed New York commander of Betar. Ignoring the Betar's leaders advice to try again for the post in a year or two, Kahane resolved to leave the organization and became its avowed enemy.

In 1948, after the establishment of the State of Israel, the Jewish Agency began funding the Betar organization. A delegation of the Betar leadership in New York, including the regional commander Morton Dolinsky, came to the Agency offices to clarify why the allocation which had been approved had never reached their office. The Jewish Agency officials were taken by surprise; they explained that Meir Kahane, presenting himself as a central figure in Betar, had already come and taken the money. He had even gone so far as to warn the Jewish Agency officials that the legitimate Betar leaders, specifically Dolinsky and the Betar treasurer Mordechai Krainer, were imposters, and would take the allocation for themselves.

Betar's main source of funding at the time came from its summer camps in the Catskill Mountains. Kahane resolved to get his hands on this money as well. He obtained a copy of the list of parents who sent their children to the camps. He told the parents the Betar camps were being reorganized, under his management, and urged them to enroll the children in his camps.

The real Betar leadership quickly exposed Kahane's actions. Their anger at his deceitful misappropriation of funds was exceeded only by their rage at his revealing internal Revisionist politics to their rivals in the Jewish Agency, controlled by the Mapai party. They warned Kahane, calling him a "thief" and a "traitor." Kahane ignored their warnings, and continued to send fliers to the parents with requests for money. He collected payments of hundreds of dollars from each family.

After Kahane ignored the Betar leaders' warnings for the third time, they decided to take more direct action. They put Kahane under surveillance. When Kahane went to a dance at a Brooklyn community center, five Betar leaders came as well. They called Kahane to come out of the building, threw him in their automobile, and sped away. They covered Kahane's head with a handkerchief, and drove him around for three hours, without saying a word. They brought him to the apartment of one of the kidnappers, where they put him on "trial." They found him guilty of informing on them to their political enemies, and of stealing movement funds. They told him that they were suspending his just punishment for the present and released him, after giving him subway fare.

Two days later Kahane's five captor-judges and three other Betar leaders were arrested at two a.m. The Brooklyn District Attorney, Eddie Silver, vented his rage on the youthful lawbreakers, but didn't start formal proceedings against them. The Betar leaders weren't surprised. They had been informed of the impending arrest by an informer they had planted among Kahane's people. Once again, Kahane was accused of informing on those who had been his comrades in the past.

Kahane married Libby Bloom in 1955. In order to pay for his studies at Brooklyn College, as well as to support his family, Kahane became a newspaper distributor. After being ordained in 1957, he served as rabbi of a synagogue in Howard Beach in Queens. Kahane's unyielding Orthodoxy ran against the trend of the times, when many Orthodox synagogues became more liberal and joined the Conservative movement. He soon found himself without a job, when he already had a wife and two children. He didn't fare much better in a later attempt to serve as a pulpit rabbi in the late 1960's, after he had already founded the Jewish Defense League. He served as the rabbi of the Traditional Synagogue in Rochedale Village, but the board of the synagogue feared reprisals by black militants for Kahane's provocations against blacks; Kahane soon left this post, claiming that running the JDL didn't leave him enough time.

During the mid-1950's he kept his job as newspaper distributor. When a strike broke out once, and there were no newspapers to distribute, the rabbi who was fired for his unbending Orthodoxy got a job as sportswriter for the *Brooklyn Daily*, winning the Grantland Rice Newspaper Sportswriting Award for his writing in 1958. Shalom Klass, the publisher of both the *Brooklyn Daily* and the Orthodox *Jewish Press*, took an interest in the gifted writer; Kahane was to become one of the main writers for the *Jewish Press*. Kahane wrote his sports columns under a variety of pseudonyms. One of them, Michael King, would later serve him as cover for activities even farther removed from the world of the Talmud.

4

A Double Life

The next decade, from the late 1950's through the late 1960's, is shrouded in mystery. Kahane does not volunteer many details of this period in his life – with good reason.

In the early 1960's the Kahane family moved to Laurelton, Queens, purchasing a house with the $10,000 Kahane received as compensation after being fired from the Howard Beach synagogue. His neighbors were impressed by the young rabbi's industriousness: distributing newspapers early in the morning, continuing during the day with his studies at the Mir Yeshivah, and finally studying law in the evening.

In order to supplement his income, Kahane also gave private Talmud classes to 8- to 12-year-olds before their Bar Mitzvah. One of his students was Eliot, the eldest son of Fred Horowitz, a wealthy industrialist. Horowitz praised Kahane's skills as a teacher, and the two men became friends.

Horowitz, a frequent visitor in the Kahane home, began to suspect that Kahane was leading a double life. On the one hand, a rabbi and family man, who earned a living from distributing newspapers and writing a sports column under a variety of pseudonyms; on the other – a figure enveloped in mystery.

From conversations overheard in Kahane's home, Horowitz surmised that Kahane was involved in supplying information to federal agencies on anti-American activities by both the left and the right. He heard the name George Rockwell, head of the American Nazi Party, mentioned in several telephone conversations and suspected that Kahane was directing other agents who were following the neo-Nazi leader. Horowitz eventually learned that Kahane was employed as a clandestine consultant by the House un-American Activities Committee. (The Committee ultimately found Kahane's testimony unsubstantiated and unconvincing.)

It was also in Kahane's home that Horowitz met Joseph Churba. Churba told Horowitz that he ran a research institute in Washington, conducting political and defense studies for federal agencies. The studies were conducted by Churba and were written up by Kahane. In 1966, they suggested that Horowitz join them, setting up an equal partnership to be funded by Horowitz.

Dazzled, Horowitz agreed, contributing $20,000. The partnership and the organization were a fiction. When Horowitz realized that he had been swindled, he demanded his money back. Churba agreed to make restitution, paying him back $10,000 over a period of two years. Kahane paid back only $5,000, half of what he owed. Horowitz took him to court where Kahane was ordered to repay the remaining money. Kahane ignored the court order and has never repaid the debt. Horowitz decided not to pursue the matter. Their relationship didn't end there, and Kahane would call on Horowitz again.

At that time, Kahane was an editor with the *Jewish Press*. Using the byline of Hayim Yerushalmi, Kahane wrote a highly laudatory article about Churba, published on March 19, 1965. According to the article, Churba, an M.A. student at Columbia, was destined for a brilliant future, as glittering as that of Henry Kissinger. Kahane identified Churba as a professor of political science at Adelphi University, as well as the head of a team at the research center for international relations at Georgetown University.

He was further described as a consultant in foreign affairs, whom Washington called on occasion to participate in high-level goverment meetings. While such publicity no doubt served Kahane and Churba well in soliciting funds for their various "research projects," the truth was another matter. By 1965,

Kahane was known in non-Jewish circles as "Michael King," whom Churba introduced as "an expert in intelligence matters." Churba, himself, was not a professor at Adelphi, but a junior teaching assistant. More importantly, the "center for international relations" to which Kahane referred in his article on Churba, simply did not exist, according to Library of Congress records.

Yet Churba and Kahane were quick to make use of the publicity generated by the *Jewish Press* article. They took out a quarter-page advertisement in the now-defunct *New York Herald-Tribune* announcing the establishment of the "Fourth of July Movement." The Movement's founders presumably wanted to mobilize support for the continuation of the Vietnam war, claiming that a cessation of the war would seriously harm Israel. They stated in the advertisement that six campus branches of the organization had already been founded. In reality, the organization consisted only of Kahane and Churba. A picture of the two published in the *New York Journal-American* showed "King" Kahane. Kahane admitted some years later that the Fourth of July Movement was a fictitious organization.

Kahane's professional connection with Churba began in 1961, when they founded Consultants Research Associates. In 1963 they received a contract from the FBI to infiltrate the extreme right wing (and anti-Semitic) John Birch Society. Their main task was to uncover the Society's sources of funding. Kahane accepted the mission, and spent several months in southern California, investigating the Society's large contributors. The John Birch leaders didn't suspect that this "Christian" member of the Society was actually an ordained rabbi. He spent about two and one half years among them making contacts among the upper strata of the local population. His new friends revealed to him all the ills of contemporary American society: drugs and interracial tension. The Jews directed these two evils, according to them, by forming an international conspiracy with the goal of destroying the United States from within, so that it would fall effortlessly into the hands of the Communists.

Kahane transmitted the desired information on the Society's contributors to the FBI. The Bureau threatened to expose them by leaking their identity to the media; the threat worked, and the John Birch Society became less extreme. The JBS heads feared the embarrassment of public exposure, and made a deal with the FBI.

Kahane, also worked for the FBI on an illegal project called "Cointelpro," a supersecret group which conducted surveillance of extremist groups from both the left and right. The group was disbanded after its illegal nature was exposed.

By the mid-sixties, Kahane's double life as Michael King was firmly entrenched in New York, Washington, and Easthampton. In 1965, Churba and Kahane rented bachelor apartments on East 85th Street in Manhattan and in Easthampton, Long Island. Rented under the name of Michael King, the apartments served the two rabbis for impressing potential clients with their various projects and for entertaining young, non-Jewish women. (When Churba and Kahane/King left the Manhattan apartment at the end of 1967, they neglected paying their telephone bill of $162 – yet another of the rabbi's unpaid debts.)

Meanwhile, Kahane's wife Libby, busy raising their four children, knew nothing of her husband's double life. The family continued to live in Laurelton, with Kahane returning home for weekends.

Near his 34th birthday in 1966, Kahane met a 22-year-old Italian girl by the name of Gloria Jean D'Argenio. Gloria had left her adopted parents in Connecticut four years earlier to come to New York to pursue a modeling career. She was using the professional name of Estelle Donna Evans when Kahane, masquerading as the non-Jewish Michael King, met her. Attracted to the beautiful model, he embarked on a passionate love affair. After a few weeks, Kahane decided the affair was growing too serious and dangerous for him. At the end of July, he wrote Gloria/Donna, telling her the affair was over.

Her response was immediate and tragic. While walking with her roommate along the Queensborough Bridge at 4:30 a.m. on July 30, Gloria hurled herself over the safety rail into the East River, 135 feet below. She was still alive and conscious when two policemen on patrol pulled her out of the water and rushed her to Lincoln Hill Hospital. She told them that she had lost all hope after reading the letter from her lover, breaking off their relationship. She died two days later, on August 1, 1966 (coincidentally, Kahane's 34th birthday).

Kahane and his followers misrepresented the circumstances of the suicide in a variety of ways over the years. To this day, his followers maintain that she had a terminal case of cancer.

Two years after the event, Kahane once more turned to Fred Horowitz, confiding that a young woman by the name of Estelle Donna Evans, who had worked as a secretary for Churba and him in Washington, had committed suicide. Kahane wanted to found a charitable foundation in her name and needed some distinguished people to serve on its board of directors. Horowitz recalls that Kahane appeared to be in a terrible state. He did not elaborate on the circumstances of the suicide, mentioning only that the young woman had been an adopted child. Horowitz gathered that Kahane had involved himself in a delicate affair and decided not to embarrass him by asking for details. He agreed to help Kahane and served as president of the foundation, with one of Horowitz's friends serving as vice-president.

Some years later, when Kahane was asked about the foundation, he replied that it had been founded and financed by the young woman's wealthy parents. Needless to say, her parents were not wealthy. It was Kahane himself who solicited contributions in JDL publications. He claimed that the foundation received about $20,000 in contributions, which were distributed to the needy in Israel. But no documentation exists to support his claim.

The young woman's mother recalls that Kahane attended Gloria's funeral in Connecticut, introducing himself as Michael King. From time to time, he would bring flowers to her daughter's grave. She had always known of the affair between them, the mother remarked. Yet when Kahane was asked about the affair in 1984, he screamed that it was "slander" and reiterated his claim that Estelle had only been his and Churba's secretary. Churba, however, denied this and underscored her romantic relationship with Kahane.

Estelle's roommate also recalled that King had a love affair with the model. She emphasized that the girl committed suicide

28

immediately after she received the letter from "King."

Kahane's love affair would have remained a secret if he had not gotten into trouble with the United States government and its law enforcement agencies. In 1971, they leaked information about Kahane to the media. On January 24, 1971, the *New York Times* was the first to contain broad hints about the affair, as part of a generally unfavorable picture of Kahane's personality. The *Times* article, the first to reveal this side of the "fighting rabbi's" character, only revealed the tip of the iceberg. The newspaper's investigators disclosed a great deal about Kahane; in a moment of weakness, Kahane had admitted to his interviewers that he had even proposed marriage to the girl. He revealed that he had led a double life, that of rabbi and communal leader during the day, while at night he walked the streets of Manhattan in search of girls. After Kahane pled with the newspaper, according to his former associates, most of the titillating details of his life were omitted from the article.

Had the *Times* revealed the entire truth about Kahane, it is quite likely that the disclosure would have effectively ended his public career. The *Times* editors incorrectly assumed that the unfavorable article, with its hints at hidden scandals, would suffice to restrain Kahane. In fact, the article had the opposite effect on his followers, who treated him as a hero; at a JDL meeting in 1971, some time after the article appeared, his followers clapped him on the shoulder and called him "a real man."

Until 1967, when cutbacks in the federal budget led to its closing, Kahane directed the Center for Political Studies in Washington, a private research organization. Churba and Kahane worked for the FBI, the CIA, and the Pentagon. Churba was later to serve as the chief advisor on Middle East Affairs for the United States Air Force. Kahane and Churba shared the same right-ring political views, including unqualified support for the Vietnam war. Kahane roundly denounced radicals, but also criticized the anti-Semitic right and the New Left. He classified himself as "left of center" since he supported federal involvement in social welfare (possibly because of his own dependence upon contributions for his needs, and to further his battles).

In 1967, Kahane and Churba wrote *The Jewish Stake in Vietnam* under the names of "Meir Kahane, Joseph Churba, and Michael King." The Kahane-Churba partnership was marked by a string of dismal failures. Their book on Vietnam, which Kahane admitted in 1971 had been financed by the American government, sold only 3,000 copies. They planned to publish a book on the political and social life of North Vietnam, but the project was scrapped after a year and a half. They tried their hand at publishing a scandal sheet on the night life of diplomats in Washington, but it ceased publication after two issues. Kahane testified before Congressional committees on Soviet Jewry and on extreme right- and left-wing organizations.

At the end of 1967 Kahane stopped spending much of his time in Washington, and based himself in New York. The reason for the move was quite prosaic: his partner Churba severed his relations with him. Their parting was not amicable. I wrote to Churba in 1985, and asked him about the reasons for the split. Churba refused to talk about Kahane, claiming that any additional publicity about Kahane would be detrimental to Israel. Sources in New York provided a different reason, stating that the two had broken relations because of a personal quarrel over a woman that Kahane introduced to Churba.

5

Origins of the JDL

In 1967, the Jews of Laurelton, including Meir Kahane and Fred Horowitz, were worried by the Middle East situation and the war clouds looming on the horizon. The statement by the Israel Defense Forces' chief chaplain, Shlomo Goren, on the need to prepare mass graves in the parks of Israel's cities, in anticipation of the high casualties expected in the war with the Arabs, deeply troubled Kahane. He warned of a second Holocaust, but did not follow the many American Jews who volunteered to aid Israel. Horowitz recalls that Kahane was no longer the same Talmud teacher that he had known. Kahane's conduct, opinions, and responses had all become much more extreme. It was impossible to carry on a normal conversation with him.

Kahane could relax only after the Israeli victory in the Six-Day War in June. He resolved to make the most of the Israeli victory.

Meanwhile, unsettling events in New York played on Jews' vulnerabilities and fears. Blacks had begun to organize to protest their second-class status. The black Panthers were born; rhetoric grew more militant; racial tensions increased. New York City schools were in a turmoil. Blacks charged that New York City's Board of Education deliberately discriminated against them and that white teachers (many of whom were Jewish) shared no common language with their black students.

Teaching and administrative staffs were predominantly white, while the student body was predominantly black. Militancy was particularly high in Brooklyn's Ocean Hill-Brownsville school system where groups called for the replacement of white school principals and teachers by blacks. Charges of black anti-Semitism proliferated. The central Board's authority was challenged and the move for local control of schools precipitated the New York City teachers' strike of 1968.

It was against this background that the Jewish Defense League was established.

At Sabbath afternoon services in May 1968, Meir Kahane outlined his plan for the defense organization to two of his fellow worshippers, Morton Dolinsky and Bertram Zweibon. After services, the three went to Dolinsky's home, where Kahane elaborated on his plan for a defense organization to protect Jews.

Dolinsky was willing to cooperate with Kahane, despite the enmity between the two men that was sparked by Kahane's kidnapping by Betar in 1952. After an unsuccessful attempt to settle in Israel during the '50's, Dolinsky had returned to his career in public relations in the United States. At the time of the Sabbath meeting in his home, Dolinsky was head of the F.L. Bacon public relations firm. He later emigrated to Israel, serving as director of the Government Press Office under Prime Minister Begin.

Zweibon was a wealthy lawyer, the son of a leading American Communist who had returned to traditional Judaism, and the nephew of a leading member of the Revisionist Zionist movement in the U.S. (The manner in which Zweibon greeted me when I interviewed him testifies to his personality. The building in which his office is located, behind the New York Public Library, is closed to anyone who doesn't identify himself. I entered the waiting room in his office. A glass wall divides the waiting area from Zweibon's office. A young woman asked me to wait. When she led me to Zweibon, he said, in a loud voice, "She isn't Jewish, but she works for me." When I asked him why he was so protected, he replied with an ear-shattering shout, "So that the police, the Mossad, or the [Israel] General

Security Services won't be able to come in to me without prior warning. There's no difference between the police here and your General Security Services in Israel.")

Kahane immediately emerged as the leader of the founding triumvirate of the Jewish Defense League. Zweibon served as legal counsel Dolinsky dealt with publicity. They were soon joined by a fourth person, Chaim Bieber, a boxer, who was known for his great physical strength. Bieber was reputed to be able to lift an automobile with his bare hands. He supplied the organization with muscle and served as Kahane's bodyguard. A printshop worker, he printed the JDL's materials. Dolinsky soon left the organization to emigrate to Israel.

The Jewish Defense League was incorporated in New York State in July 1968. Its charter listed the JDL's goals: "To combat anti-Semitism in the public and private sectors of life in the United States of America; to uphold and defend the Constitution of the United States of America; to support all agencies of government charged with the responsibility of maintaining law and order; to foster a sense of obligation by the individual to the community, state and nation; to safeguard and transmit to posterity the principles of justice, freedom and democracy."

By now, the New York City teachers' strike had erupted, amidst a welter of charges and countercharges – many of them racially and ethnically tinged – that often obscured the real issues involved: those of local vs. central control of the city's schools.

Kahane was now an editor of the *Jewish Press*, which had a circulation of 130,000 to 160,000. He was flooded with telephone calls and letters complaining about attacks on Jewish teachers resulting from racial incitement in the schools, about attacks on Jews in general and muggings. Some Jewish cemeteries were desecrated on Halloween and blacks were accused of vandalism in Kahane's own all-white community of Laurelton. The general press did not report many of these attacks on Jews if there were no real casualties.

Kahane was quick to reap the fruits of this apparent rise in anti-Semitism. He viciously attacked John Lindsay in his campaign for reelection as mayor. One of the JDL's first actions was to protect local Jewish cemeteries. JDL members, equipped with clubs, patrolled Jewish neighborhoods in cars with two-way radios. They set up ambushes. The would-be vandals, seeing that the JDL patrols were waiting for them, fled. After this initial success, the patrols were extended to ensure the safety of Jews walking in mixed neighborhoods.

In an attempt to gain support and legitimization from the Jewish establishment, Kahane launched "Operation Hagana" to ensure safety in the streets of Jewish neighborhoods. He requested eight national Jewish organizations to establish a $100,000 fund for the purchase of automobiles and the hiring of guards to patrol on foot, equipped with walkie-talkies. Arnold Forster of the Anti-Defamation League, summed up Kahane's initiative in one word: "Chutzpah."

In practice, there was no continuity to the patrols. No patrols lasted more than two weeks. Most of the patrols were the result of on-the-spot, sporadic planning, without any organized duty rosters.

Kahane was quick to turn the appeals for help which he received into an instrument for his own publicity. He turned to the heads of the major Jewish organizations with the appeals, and asked them how they intended to respond. As usual, he exaggerated the anti-Semitic threat, and the Jewish leaders were not especially moved by him. They advised him to act with restraint; they felt that any violent response would lead to an escalation of anti-Semitic attacks and advised keeping a low profile. Kahane replied that he didn't intend to offer the other cheek; silence would only intensify the problem. He decided to take action. With his newspaper at his disposal, he ran an advertisement. Under the headline, "We are talking of Jewish Survival," he asked, "Are you willing to stand up for democracy and Jewish survival? Join and support the Jewish Defense Corps." He included a membership application, with dues set at $10. The advertisement ran on May 24, 1968, a few weeks before the organization applied for incorporation. The next week the newspaper (i. e., Kahane) announced that $200,000 had been collected in response to the advertisement. Kahane decided to ride the wave of this success and published many articles, written under a variety of names (such as Meir Hacohen), congratulating himself.

The change in the Jewish self-image and the wave of increased Jewish pride after the Israeli victory in the Six-Day War also contributed to Kahane's success. The wave of anti-Semitism, the raison d'etre of the JDL, subsided, just as the Jewish leaders (who had been derisively rejected by Kahane) had predicted.

Apart from the JDL's official aims, set out in the organization's charter, Kahane set three goals for himself: Jewish pride, Jewish self-defense, and Jewish political power. He wanted to change the Jewish self-image, which appeared to him to be servile and obsequious. He declared that the JDL would prevent young anti-Semites from robbing Jewish schoolchildren of their lunch money. He derisively stated that Jews always fight for the rights of blacks and Puerto Ricans, and for grapes, lettuce, and Vietnam; the time had come for Jews to act on their own behalf. If black was beautiful, then Jewish was beautiful too.

Officially, Kahane was number one in the organization, Zweibon was number two, and there was a five-member Executive Board and a twelve-member National Board. In practice, Kahane called all the shots; there was never internal democracy in the JDL. In 1970 the JDL adopted its slogan, "Never Again." Kahane, who had always craved publicity, found that his new organization suited his needs perfectly. The Jewish Defense League was more of an ongoing publicity stunt than a serious organizational development. It served as a vehicle for young Jewish toughs who were looking for excitement, and who wanted an opportunity to vent their frustrations and prove their masculinity to competing minorities in New York's mixed neighborhoods. Unlike his earlier failures with Churba, the JDL was an instant success, providing Kahane with much material for his column in the *Jewish Press*, covering whole pages every week.

The JDL's main bases were in the Jewish neighborhoods of Borough Park and Flatbush in Brooklyn, Laurelton in Queens, neighborhoods in the Bronx, and the lower East Side of Manhattan. Kahane was never popular in the Hasidic neighborhoods of Crown Heights and Williamsburg in Brooklyn. Those closed communities relied on their rabbis, who shunned publicity. They had preceded Kahane in setting up their own self-defense organizations, which effectively protected their neighborhoods, without Kahane's publicity, which they found offensive.

In May 1969 James Forman, a militant black civil rights leader, threatened to appear at New York's prestigious Temple Emanu-El, as he had at major churches, demanding "compensation" for the suffering blacks had endured at the hands of whites, both Jews and Christians. The leaders of the temple didn't ask for the JDL's protection; Kahane didn't consult them. Young JDL members positioned themselves at the entrance to the temple, armed with clubs and chains, but Forman disappointed them – he didn't show up. A few years later, JDL members themselves were to make the same demands as Forman. In 1973, Kahane's people went into the offices of the World Council of Churches and demanded a grant – actually protection money – of $25,000. In 1975, they even took over Temple Emanu-El.

Kahane initially drew much of his support from teenagers, most of whom came from lower-income families in Queens and the Bronx. Kahane always had a way with young people. As a teacher, he could fascinate his pupils with stories and dreams about the Redemption of the Jews and the Messiah. Many of those joining the JDL were Kahane's own pupils in the schools and yeshivot in which he taught. Joining the JDL provided an opportunity to express themselves in a manner which membership in other Jewish organizations did not. The JDL gave them a chance to rebel against their parents, the Jewish establishment, and American society as a whole. Membership in the JDL (as in Kach in Israel today) also contained elements of belonging to a secret, underground organization. There were classes in karate for self-defense, and training with weapons during paramilitary exercises in the League's closed camps in the Catskills. These teenagers were suddenly treated as adults, with responsibility and missions. They had been adrift in a non-Jewish world; now they returned to their Jewish roots (as interpreted by Kahane). The violence repressed within them for years now had an outlet; they had power to use and targets to eliminate. They discovered their Jewishness and revelled in the triumphs of the Israel Defense Forces – "their" army. They had a "fighting rabbi," a prophetic, almost Messianic figure, as their leader, one who was persecuted by the authorities and reviled by the conservative Jewish establishment. The JDL had a definite masculine orientation, but women also joined, and made their way to the leadership level of the organization.

Kahane adopted tactics which had been developed by the radical movements of the New Left on campuses in Europe and America. Kahane was the sole determiner of policy, and still is today, even though the JDL has deteriorated to a mailing address, an automatic answering device, and several hooligans willing to carry out Kahane's provocations when he comes to the United States. The JDL had never been run by an orderly, controlled policy. Its many sudden changes of course, from one project to the next, reflected changes in its leader's thinking. Kahane projects are seldom carefully thought out. As a result, his actions, both in America and Israel, never attain their declared goals, but rather serve Kahane's need for publicity.

The composition of Kahane's followers changes with the times. When the JDL was in its infancy in 1968, he was supported by those Jewish teachers who felt threatened by black anti-Semitism. He was also supported by Russian Jewish emigres who viewed him as a hero. They soon left him, giving their support to traditional political parties and established Jewish organizations. The teachers were repelled by his violent methods and dictatorial personality. His aggressive actions against leaders of the Jewish establishment, who devoted their lives to serving the Jewish people, also caused many of his original followers to abandon him. In the final analysis, Kahane is always left with those on the fringes of society: teenagers from broken homes; drug addicts; *ba'alei teshuvah* – Jews who have recently returned to Orthodox Judaism and have abandoned their former lifestyles; residents of deteriorating neighborhoods in the United States and of development towns in Israel; the unemployed; Arab haters; the unbalanced, looking for action.

Street patrols soon gave way to sheer violence and vandalism. JDL members, armed with baseball bats and motorcycle chains, caused disturbances in Jewish neighborhoods. They shouted and emptied trashcans on the sidewalk. They even vandalized synagogues and Jewish cemeteries, attacking the very Jews they were supposed to be defending, in order to "prove" the existence of anti-Semitism. Former members of the JDL relate that Williamsburg Jews had to ask JDL members to leave the neighborhood because they were exacerbating an incident in which a drunken Jewish driver had run over and killed a black girl, leading to interracial tension which had not existed in the neighborhood before the appearance of the JDL. At the end of the 1960's and the beginning of the 1970's, JDL provocateurs sent threatening letters to Jews in order to increase immigration to Israel (while the senders of the letters themselves remained in the United States). Kahane would later send similar letters to Arabs in Israel, in order to encourage them to emigrate. JDL members who had been ordered to immigrate to Israel to form cadres for Kahane, who had promised to follow them, were labeled "traitors" and "cowards" if they decided to remain in the United States.

Jewish and Israeli institutions were not immune to JDL vandalism. In order to avoid legal action, the JDL paid $1500 to the New York Board of Rabbis for damages caused by its members to the Board's offices. Six of the JDL's toughs took over the offices of the San Francisco Jewish Federation, threw out the federation's employees, broke into file cabinets, and destroyed furniture. The Israeli Consul-General in New York, Paul Kedar, was forced to call the police to evict JDL members who had waged a sit-down strike in the consulate.

Kahane apparently preferred provocative actions that would elicit headlines to effective long range projects that might better benefit Jewish neighborhoods, the Jewish poor, and Soviet Jewry.

6

The JDL and Soviet Jewry

To be sure, Meir Kahane was not the first to take action on behalf of Soviet Jewry. Other Jewish organizations and individuals had preceded him by many years. Their nonviolent efforts had already put the issue in the headlines. Kahane adopted the cause of Soviet Jewry only in December 1969 and began activities in 1970. Unlike other protest organizations, Kahane employed violent and repellent methods, which alienated many of his earlier followers.

Among those organizations that first called attention to the plight of Jews in the Soviet Union were the Student Struggle for Soviet Jewry, founded in New York in 1964, and the Soviet Jewry Action Group, founded in California in 1969.

Yaakov Birnbaum, one of the founders and the head of the Student Struggle for Soviet Jewry, was the first to focus public attention on Soviet Jewry. The Student Struggle, founded in 1964 in New York, set out to place the issue of Soviet Jewry on the Jewish and general American agenda. It produced educational materials on the issue, and provided speakers for synagogues, churches, and educational institutions. It exerted constant, ever-increasing pressure on major Jewish organizations to take positive action. The cases of individual "refuseniks" who had been denied permission to emigrate to Israel and Prisoners of Zion in Soviet prisons and labor camps were given much publicity. This publicity provided these individuals with a measure of protection from Soviet harassment; many of them were eventually released from prison and permitted to emigrate. Mass demonstrations, such as the annual Passover Seder held outside the Soviet mission to the UN, became a tradition for many New Yorkers.

Paralleling and complementing the actions of the SSSJ, Jerry Westin, a graduate student at Berkeley, founded the Soviet Jewry Action Group in 1969. The SJAG, and the Union of Councils for Soviet Jewry umbrella organization, which included close to 20 local organizations such as the SJAG, pioneered such activities as sending of New Year's greeting cards to individual Soviet Jews. A protest organized by the SJAG during the October 27, 1969 visit to San Francisco by Soviet cosmonauts, and the painting of the slogan "Let the Jews Out" on a Soviet freighter anchored in San Francisco harbor on January 26, 1970, received wide media coverage. The SJAG conducted mass demonstrations such as a candlelight vigil at the new Soviet consulate in San Francisco. More than 10 percent of the San Francisco Jewish community would eventually participate in SJAG-organized activities. Distinguished figures, including Nobel Prize laureates, participated in SJAG activities. The UCSJ also published *Exodus*, a monthly newspaper with news from the Soviet Union and reports on protest activities.

Such activities were initially opposed by the Jewish establishment, following the lead of the Israeli government led by Prime Minister Golda Meir, who preferred quiet diplomacy. Eventually, the Jewish establishment would adopt many of the forms of protest initiated by the Student Struggle for Soviet Jewry and the Union of Councils for Soviet Jewry. As a result, the issue became a major one in American politics, culminating in the Jackson-Vanik amendment concerning America's foreign trade: the United States officially linked the granting of trade benefits to the USSR with free immigration from the Soviet Union. Hundreds of thousands of Soviet Jews were permitted to leave the USSR as a result of the concerted activity on their behalf.

Yaakov Birnbaum did not regard Meir Kahane's activities on behalf of Soviet Jewry as being of great importance. Kahane had indeed called for concrete action on behalf of Soviet Jewry in his articles in the *Jewish Press* in 1964, and had demonstrated in front of the Soviet mission to the UN in New York, but his involvement went no further. Nor was Kahane troubled by the issue after the founding of the Jewish Defense League in 1968. Soviet Jewry was not mentioned in any of the JDL's publications or propaganda. A 14-page booklet listing the JDL's goals and aims, written in 1969, did not mention the subject of the Jews of Silence. A 29-page booklet on the League's principles and philosophies, written during the same period, devoted only a few sentences to the issue.

As publicity for JDL's defense of Jewish neighborhoods waned, Kahane's interest in Soviet Jewry rose. He initiated action with no acknowledgement to the work of those who had preceded him.

One of the heads of the JDL at the time recalled how the JDL was informed of the issue: "Kahane came to the office one day with a new idea in his head. He announced the change in the League's goals. Several members of the board did not understand what he was talking about, since his new project wasn't covered in the League's platform or publications." The JDL's brutal actions on behalf of Soviet Jewry continued for about a year and a half, until Kahane emigrated to Israel.

On June 15, 1970, 11 Jews and 2 non-Jews were arrested in Leningrad as they were about to hijack a small plane and fly it to Israel. A few days later, the KGB arrested an additional 20 Jews who had signed petitions for exit permits to Israel. The alleged hijackers were charged with treason. The arrests and the ensuing stiff sentences led to an immediate outburst of protest throughout the world, with the active participation of the Jewish establishment.

Kahane decided to milk the issue for its publicity value. Twenty-seven JDL activists took over the Lexington Avenue offices of Amtorg, the Soviet trading corporation, evicting the 25 employees on the 19th and 20th stories of the building. The press appeared; the media was full of Kahane and his actions. Kahane increased his pressure on the Soviets, holding demonstrations and prayer vigils (as did other Jewish organizations; the difference between the two was the violence of the JDL actions). The JDL even put bombs in Soviet installations in New York.

When Kahane realized that his actions were not received favorably by the White House, he indirectly threatened President Nixon. At a large demonstration held by the JDL in Washington on March 21, 1971, Kahane told his followers: "The JDL is convinced that President Nixon, who holds the key to saving Soviet Jewry, doesn't give two damns about the Soviet Jewish problem. Obviously, the next step is to take the Jewish problem and make it Richard Nixon's problem." The *Washington Post* reported on March 1, 1971 that Kahane also said, "We're trying to drive Richard Nixon so crazy with worrying about Jews bothering him, he'll tell the Russians, 'Look, I've got this Jewish problem and we can't go any further with trade and cultural exchanges until you let the Jews go'."

Kahane tried to involve the major Jewish organizations in his demonstrations, but they were repelled by his violent ways. Because of his rejection by the Jewish establishment, the pressure of trials pending against him and his fear of imprisonment, Kahane decided to halt his campaign of harassment against the Soviets. Preparating for a demonstration in Washington, he formed the Student Activists for Soviet Jewry, one of a dozen front groups he founded during the JDL's career. He thought that the new group would serve as a quasi-underground extension of the JDL, assuming the responsibility for the League's illegal activities. Partly for convenience, but mainly due to his fear of imprisonment, Kahane wanted to separate the new organization from the JDL. Evading the police by hiding behind a front group was standard operating procedure for Kahane.

On February 14, 1971, a few weeks before the demonstration in Washington, Kahane tried to heat up the atmosphere by proclaiming an end to the moratorium on those violent actions he had previously endorsed. Only a few Jewish organizations (Young Israel, Noar Mizrachi, and Betar) responded to Kahane's call to donate money or participate in the Washington demonstration. The major Jewish organizations, as well as the Student Struggle for Soviet Jewry, recognized that the "Student

Activists" was just a vehicle for Kahane, and refused to participate.

A few days before the demonstration, the JDL ran advertisement in the *New York Times*. Under a picture of a pile of bodies in Auschwitz, the advertisement read "This is the price of silence... 1943, when we knew that 12,000 Jews were daily being shipped to Auschwitz aboard cattle car trains... and could have been saved by bombing the rail lines to the death camps – we were silent! ... Because of that silence over 6,000,000 died! Never again can we be silent in the face of another Jewish tragedy! Come with us to the White House, Sunday... You can help free Soviet Jewry if you get off your apathy."

On Sunday, 1,000 people assembled in New York and went to Washington in 28 buses.

Three thousand demonstrators gathered to hear Kahane speak. "Few people care about a Jewish problem," he told them, "but the whole world goes to any lengths to solve a world problem. We are gathered in Washington to give the world a king-sized headache." (*Washington Post*, March 22, 1971.)

More than a headache ensued when Kahane, in a sudden shift of plans, ordered his demonstrators to stage a sit-down at the intersection of K and 16th Streets, close to the Soviet Embassy. The Washington police wanted to avert the sit-down, but Kahane persisted.

Jerry Wilson, Washington chief of police, told William Perl, head of the JDL in Washington, "tell Rabbi Kahane that he has had all the publicity he wants. This was all filmed and will be on television. If you continue on your prearranged route there will be no arrests." Kahane told Perl to "Tell Chief Wilson that we will be sitting here until either the very last Jew is released from the Soviet Union or the very last of us is arrested." Perl condensed this to, "I'm very sorry, the rabbi said he can't do that." Kahane was primarily interested in the publicity which would follow mass arrests; the struggle for Jewish emigration from the USSR was incidental. The police warned that arrests would begin if the demonstrators did not clear the streets. Kahane told the demonstrators, "You will survive an arrest. If 5,000 people get arrested it will be on page one of the newspapers; otherwise it will be next to the obituary column. Thirty years ago while Hitler turned Jews into soap, we did nothing when President Roosevelt said he couldn't help. We didn't even do what Martin Luther King did for his people. Now we have an opportunity to help our Jewish brothers who are crying out to us. Feel their pain. The Jews in the Soviet Union have it so much worse. They sat down in Parliament Square in Moscow and they weren't afraid, so don't you be afraid to sit down here in Washington. After they're arrested in Russia, they're sent to forced labor camps. Here, Jews have marched for every one else's rights – for blacks, even for Eskimos. It is time to shake up the world a bit for Jews."

The emotional appeal by Kahane, and by Yossi Templeman, one of the chief organizers of the demonstration, convinced the demonstrators to sit down. Kahane also emphasized that violence was to be avoided, and told the demonstrators to cooperate with the police. Kahane was the first to be arrested.

Carl Bernstein (co-author of the Watergate expose *All the President's Men*), covered the demonstration for the *Washington Post*. Bernstein wrote: "As he led the young man away to be arrested, the patrolman turned to his sergeant, then whispered, 'I kind of hate to do it; these kids are different.' Indeed, aside from their youth, the determined army of Jews who sat down in the streets near the Soviet Embassy yesterday bore few resemblances to demonstrators with whom Washington's police are more accustomed to dealing. Yesterday, there were no fashionable uniforms of the revolution just purchased at some neighborhood liberation boutique, no shouts of 'off the pigs,' no thrown stones, no chanted obscenities, no gas masks, red flags or dialectical rhetoric." (March 22, 1971.) *Pravda* was not so sympathetic; its Washington correspondent described the demonstration as the "hooligan actions of the Zionist Organization."

Over one thousand three hundred demonstrators were arrested. In addition to making page one headlines in major American newspapers, Kahane made Washington history; this was the largest number of demonstrators to be arrested in a single demonstration in the capital city. Five hours after he was

44

released from jail in Washington, Kahane declared that "Jews are so obsessed with respectability that we constantly have on our minds the question: If we are not respectable, what will non-Jews say? It is about time that we buried respectability before it buries us."

Only a week passed before Kahane's followers bombed the offices of the Communist Party on March 30.

7

Kahane and the Mafia

Kahane received substantial aid from the New York Mafia. The first real link between Meir Kahane and Joseph (Joe) Colombo, a Mafia figure in New York, was formed in May 1971, when Kahane was in jail on a charge of illegal possesson of weapons and explosives. He wanted to be freed on bail, but the JDL treasury was empty, as usual. Imprisonment drove Kahane mad. He had always feared it and done everything (even informing on his comrades to the authorities) in order to avoid going to jail. Kahane knows that he can attract publicity only when he is free.

Nine other JDL activists were imprisoned along with Kahane. In 1972 Kahane stated that a total of $155,000 out of a budget of $250,000 was spent on their bail. In order to leave jail as quickly as possible, Kahane was willing to make a pact with the devil himself.

Kahane's criminal lawyer was Barry Slotnick, one of the leading criminal lawyers in New York, who was also Joe Colombo's lawyer. Kahane asked Slotnick to make the connection with the Mafia leader. Kahane's arrest attracted the attention of the media. He found the attention flattering, but the imprisonment unbearable. Colombo listened attentively to Slotnick, who told him that Kahane wanted Colombo's help in raising bail. Colombo jumped at the opportunity. He replied that Kahane was a man after his own heart, a man "fighting for

46

his people." As a veteran Mafioso, Colombo could appreciate Kahane's violent methods. He realized he could use Kahane to improve his own image; public disclosure of the link between the two would benefit Colombo. He immediately agreed to provide bail for all the prisoners.

Colombo and his son Anthony, his chief aide, sat in the first row of the Federal Court in Brooklyn. Judge Max Shifman ruled that Kahane would be released upon the posting of $25,000 bail, while the other detainees, including Kahane's bodyguard Chaim Bieber and Irving Calderone, one of the heads of the JDL, were to be released upon $10,000 bail. The presence of Colombo as Kahane's current patron aroused the interest of the media. A photograph taken when the two left the courtroom shows them standing on the stairs of the court, smiling broadly and looking quite pleased with themselves. The photographers didn't stop taking pictures, and the reporters present rained a steady stream of questions. Colombo said that "Rabbi Kahane is a man of God, and his struggle is just." The reporters were dumbfounded. Another compliment like this and Kahane's public career would be finished for good. Colombo promised, "If they need our support, we will give it." Kahane: "We most certainly will ask him for his support." Journalist: "What's your philosophy behind this alliance?" Kahane: "I'm not a philosopher. This morning I am a defendant."

– "What about the theological implications?" Kahane: "It's human brotherhood. People of other faiths and backgrounds have come to help. It's the kind of thing which, had it been blacks helping Jews, it would have been raves. The Italians are no worse than the blacks." (As reported in the *New York Times*, May 14, 1971.)

When he was asked about this in 1972, Kahane was quick to falsify the facts. He claimed that Colombo suddenly appeared in the courtroom, offered him the services of his lawyer and paid their bail of $50,000. No Jewish rabbi did this, even though this was a case of "freeing captives" [a cardinal commandment in Judaism]. Yet Colombo helped them and didn't ask for anything in return. After Colombo's death, however, Kahane had no qualms about calling his former benefactor "a killer and criminal." Bertram Zweibon, then number two in the JDL, echoed Kahane's claim that no Jewish leader had stepped forward to help them in court, and that the Italian League offered aid on its own initiative.

Kahane clearly had no moral qualms about accepting Colombo's aid while the Mafia boss was alive. In 1971 Kahane kept quiet about the aid from Colombo until the last possible moment. There were rumors about the alliance; one reporter asked Colombo a few days before Kahane was charged whether he would provide the bail money. Colombo said he would not, adding, "Rabbi Kahane is a man of the cloth and a fine man. I am certain he will be able to post bail." On the advice of his lawyer, Colombo concealed what had been arranged in Slotnick's office. When Kahane was asked if Colombo would raise bail for him, Slotnick volunteered that bail had been provided by "friends in the community."

Kahane had known Colombo slightly even before Slotnick arranged for bail money from the Mafia leader. The previous winter Kahane had been invited to a meeting of the Italian American Civil Rights League. The senior Colombo was the founder and power behind the organization. Kahane was treated with great honor by Joe Colombo, and the Mafioso even pinned a medal on Kahane's breast.

Yossi Shneider served as the secretary- general of the JDL in Israel in the early 1970's and was one of Kahane's inner circle. He had been in the United States in 1971. During an interview in 1984, Shneider recalled that before staging a sit-down strike at the White House on behalf of Soviet Jewry, he had gone to a meeting of the Italian League with Kahane and his New York people. Shneider suggested the reasons for the strange alliance: "The Italians cheered the rabbi. During that period Kahane was fighting against John Lindsay, the New York mayor. He didn't want him for a second term. This was Colombo's position as well. The two of them found a common language and wanted to defeat Lindsay. Then Colombo got $50,000 for Kahane's bail. Kahane wanted the Russians to know that the Mafia had an alliance with him. He said that the Mafia had a name, and that the Russians would be afaid of it, and not harm the Jews.

48

Colombo's men participated in the demonstrations which the JDL held."

Kahane and Colombo developed a close relationship. Kahane enlisted Colombo's Italians for his demonstrations because he couldn't mobilize enough Jewish demonstrators. Kahane did his best to hide the fact that he couldn't mobilize enough people for his protests against the Kremlin, and that Mafia members had to fill the ranks. In return, JDL members were ordered to join the daily vigil which the Italians held in front of the FBI's offices, protesting the Bureau's "harassment" of Italians.

Relations between the two men became ever closer, and they even talked about an alliance between the two Leagues. Kahane was lavish in his praise of Colombo, presenting him as a fighter for the rights of Italians. Kahane demanded to know why he should reject Colombo's help, asking rhetorically whether the Italians were any worse than the Black Panthers, whom many Jews supported. He claimed he had asked Colombo to end the harassment of Jews in Borough Park by Italians, and that Colombo complied. Kahane compared himself to Ze'ev Jabotinsky, who had connections with the Italians, and to Mussolini. The Borough Park neighborhood, with a population of 100,000 Jews, most of them observant, had in fact been free of crime until the advent of the JDL and its hooligans. It was their provocative actions that aroused hostile reactions from the few thousand non-Jews in the area.

Just when Kahane was about to form a pact with Colombo, a commission of the New York State legislature issued a report naming Colombo "the boss," who headed one of the five Cosa Nostra "families" in New York. The report charged that Colombo was a loan shark, had stolen securities, and was involved in illegal gambling and the distribution of pornographic literature, among other crimes, in New York and other American cities. Like Kahane, Colombo was entangled in criminal cases. He was involved in the theft of diamonds worth $750,000, and faced contempt of court and perjury charges. He had been arrested on an interstate gambling charge (involving a yearly take of $10,000,000), and awaited trial on income tax evasion.

None of this seemed to bother Kahane. A contact from the Italian League was a regular visitor to the JDL's 42nd Street office. The two Leagues planned joint projects to create publicity. Anthony Colombo told reporters: "We are 100 percent in favor of the work JDL is doing." About a month before Kahane's trial was scheduled to start, Colombo's son declared that the JDL was "fighting for the civil rights of Jewish people in the Soviet Union and the United States, as we are fighting for the civil rights of our people in the United States.... We will stand with the JDL in all their demonstrations." Kahane returned the favor by speaking before 100,000 participants at Colombo's Unity Day rally. At the same time he continued to play down opposition by the Jewish establishment to his alliance with the Colombo group.

The *New York Times* summed up Kahane's decision to turn to the Mafia as "an act of desperation. As he himself acknowledges, Rabbi Kahane has been repudiated by every major Jewish organization and he finds himself now under indictment on serious charges which could send him to trial after a lengthy and expensive legal battle. In his worry about his own future, it seems not to bother Rabbi Kahane that by making such an unsavory alliance he has only provided additional reason for public revulsion against his already- discredited organization of strong-arm extremists" (May 15, 1971).

Colombo's group treated Kahane as a hero after he was charged with possession of firearms without a license – a serious offence which further distanced Kahane from the Jewish leadership. Both Kahane and Colombo were regarded as pariahs by their respective communities.

Kahane and Colombo wanted to celebrate their new alliance before the television cameras. Their first public meeting was held on a Long Island golf course. Anthony drove his father to the game in a big Cadillac. Kahane exchanged his usual black skullcap for a baseball hat with the symbol of the Italian League. Colombo pinned a JDL button proclaiming "Never Again" on his shirt. After the match the two held an impromptu press conference, ringed by their bodyguards.

It was the last publicity event of its kind. Colombo was shot at the conclusion of "Unity Day" festivities in June 1971. Kahane was accorded a special honor: he was one of the five people, and the only Jew, permitted to enter the hospital room of the mortally wounded Mafia leader. The alliance between the two Leagues faded after Colombo's death.

Kahane's critics in the United States maintain that the JDL also had ties with Meyer Lansky, the Cosa Nostra's financial wizard, and that JDL activists were used to smuggle hard drugs into the United States. When the Italian police arrested a drug smuggling ring led by Salvatore Zizzo in September 1974, Kahane's opponents charged that the Zizzo family had close ties to a JDL branch – ties that were forged by Colombo in the late sixties. The Zizzo ring was involved in smuggling drugs from the Far East to the U.S. and Canada. Many are aware that some JDL members have been addicted to drugs in both the United States and Israel. Several were charged with the use and distribution of drugs in the United States. The charges were inexplicably dropped, suggesting that they may have served as informers.

After Colombo's death, Kahane formed another questionable alliance with Dr. Thomas Matthew, the self-proclaimed leader of the black National Economic Growth and Reconstruction Organization. Matthew called Kahane proposing an alliance similar to that which Colombo's group had with the JDL. This proposal came in the wake of a violent struggle which had erupted between JDL activists and militant blacks on the Brooklyn College campus, partially resulting from JDL provocations. Speedy intervention was needed to defuse the situation. Kahane couldn't resist the temptation of the publicity to be reaped from the meeting with the black leader. The two met a week later in Harlem, inviting the press to a "peace conference", designed to ease tension between blacks and Jews. But the black leader upstaged Kahane.

At the conclusion of the short and superficial meeting, Matthew announced to reporters that the JDL was not anti-black and proposed sending a delegation of blacks to the USSR to demand that Jews be permited to emigrate. Matthew stated that he would not embarrass the Russians by asking permission for the Jews to emigrate to Israel, but would request their emigration to a neutral country for two years, during the course of which he hoped to solve the Arab-Israeli conflict. Kahane was taken by surprise by Matthew's announcement; the black had stolen the show from him and won wide coverage in the media. Instead of initiating the event, Kahane found himself swept along by Matthew. The meeting, which Kahane had called an important landmark in ethnic relations, marked the beginning and end of his new alliance.

Although he had been relatively unknown before the "peace conference," Matthew's illegal activities soon hit the news. In 1973, he was indicted on 120 criminal charges, among them the theft and misuse of hundreds of thousands of dollars in U.S. government Funds.

8

Kahane, the Soviets, and the FBI

The JDL's continuing harassment of Soviet diplomats proved a thorn for the U.S. government during a period of deterioration in Soviet-American relations. So much so, that U.S. Attorney General John Mitchell authorized the FBI to tap the telephones of Kahane and other JDL leaders. Electronic eavesdropping was conducted at JDL headquarters from October 1970 to July 1971. Nine FBI agents listened to the conversations of sixteen JDL activities on six telephone lines, in an attempt to avert attacks on Soviet diplomats in Washington and New York.

JDL counsel Bertram Zweibon brought a lawsuit against the wire taps, asking for $782,000 in damages. The government pleaded "national security," but the court found for Zweibon and awarded the sum he had requested in filing the suit on behalf of the JDL.

Although he himself had once been an FBI informer, Kahane claimed (in his book, *The Story of the Jewish Defense League*) that information on the JDL had been supplied to the FBI by B'nai B'rith's Anti-Defamation League. This was Kahane's attempt to downplay the presence of FBI agents and JDL informers in his own ranks.

Indeed, it was a JDL member, turned informer in 1971, who reported to New York City police agent Santo Parola on the JDL's plans for "full guerrilla warfare against the USSR."

Parola conveyed the information at a meeting convened by George Bush, then U.S. ambassador to the UN. The meeting, held in Bush's office at the Waldorf-Astoria, was attended by representatives from federal secret service agencies, as well as the local district attorney. Speaking for the President, Bush underscored his resolve to stop the JDL from carrying out its plans.

When asked by reporters in May 1971 about federal investigators who had questioned him, Kahane replied: "They ask me what I know about the bombing of some Soviet office or another, or about the burning of some Soviet automobile. I say that I don't know anything, offer them tea with lemon, and we talk about politics."

Yet JDL activists claimed that federal investigators learned much from Kahane himself, confirming their earlier reports from agents and informers planted in JDL branches. The information collected by the FBI proved explosive and began to be leaked to the press. Among the documents leaked was a report on the JDL, prepared by the Anti-Defamation League of B'nai B'rith.

Although Kahane was well aware that most of the FBI's material had been acquired through wiretaps and planted agents, he continually berated Jewish leaders and organizations for trying to undermine him. There was a grain of truth in his accusations. In 1969, the ADL prepared a report whose intent was to stifle the growth of the JDL by exposing the organizations's tax violations, fraud, and falsification of documents in the clandestine administration and operation of its summer camps in the Catskills. The camps served as training grounds in the use of weapons and explosives.

Meanwhile, the Justice Department speeded up the legal proceedings against Kahane and his men. The forgiving attitude which the authorities had revealed towards Kahane's earlier activities in Jewish neighborhoods was replaced by a harsher, uncompromising stance. As JDL violence increased, the authorities took an increasingly harder line against Kahane. The New York police increased their protection of Soviet installations. The Justice Department and the New York State government pressured New York Mayor John Lindsay to forcibly repress any violent conduct by Kahane and his men. Secretary of State William Rogers and U.S. Ambassador to the UN Charles Yost talked with Lindsay about the League's harassment. After Kahane had been arrested a few times for his activities on behalf of Soviet Jewry, the "fighting rabbi" hurriedly declared a moratorium on his anti-Soviet activities. After quick, concerted action by federal and local authorities, when the threat of prolonged imprisonment had become a distinct possibility, he suddenly wanted to placate the superpower upon which he had declared war. As Kahane would later write, the JDL did not want the the Russians to "lose face," because if they did, they would resist the emigration of the Jews. He wanted, therefore, to enable the Russians "to make their concessions quietly and not under duress." He even found a Biblical passage to support his sudden change of heart, citing Ecclesiastes' dictum that there is "A time for war and a time for peace." (Meir Kahane, *The Story of the Jewish Defense League*, 1975, p. 44.)

Acting on information supplied by a central JDL figure, New York City police uncovered illegal caches of arms weapons, ammunition, and explosives – purchased by JDL members under assumed names, such as David Raziel (head of the underground Tzva'i Leumi in Mandatory Palestine) and Manfred Begin.

The criminal file against Kahane grew thicker daily. In June 1971, Kahane was enmeshed in a net of criminal charges: attacks against Soviet installations; harassment of Soviet and Iraqi diplomats; possession of firearms and ammunition without a license; participation in violent demonstrations; disturbing the peace. Immigration to Israel by JDL members increased, in an attempt to flee from the trials awaiting them. Some of these JDL members would later become involved in Kahane's anti-Arab incitement in Israel. Among the more serious charges facing Kahane and his people were those of conspiracy to throw homemade Molotov cocktails, underground production of bombs, and the use of explosives. Youngsters had received arms training in JDL camps in the Catskills and other parts of the U.S. The weapons and explosives were held without license – a serious violation of federal law. In these camps veterans from the American and Israeli armies instructed the campers, not only in karate for self-defense, but also in the use of weapons, the production of bombs, Molotov cocktails, grenades, small tin-can napalm bombs, mines, etc. They also took steps to purchase mortars and bazookas. Kahane wanted to create a "new Jew," in the footsteps of the heroes of the Bible. The camps combined lessons in Jewish history with preparation for street fighting.

Much of this was uncovered by Richard Rosenthal, an agent planted in the JDL by the New York Police Department's Bureau of Special Investigations. Rosenthal, 22 years old, had served for four years in U.S. Air force intelligence. He joined the JDL in 1969 and managed to infiltrate the top echelon of the organization This placed him in a position to gain firsthand knowledge of activities in the JDL summer camps. The camps' nine-week summer course of intensive exercises began each day at 5 a.m. and included karate, weapons instruction, practice shooting with real ammunition, swimming, horseback riding, running obstacle courses, placing mines, and producing Molotov cocktails and bombs. The JDL was reputed to have stolen large quantities of arms, mostly mortars and bazookas, from U.S. Army warehouses and bases abroad. Reports also sugested that they had smuggled arms, among them small mobile rockets, from the IDF to JDL bases in Europe and America.

According to senior sources within the JDL, Kahane had been warned that Rosenthal was an agent, but chose to ignore the warnings. Meanwhile, Rosenthal reported that the JDL had made contacts in Israel for smuggling Israeli Uzi submachine guns and Swedish Karl Gustav guns. An ex-IDF soldier called "Dov" was reputed to have been recruited by Avraham Herskovitz, a leading JDL figure, to provide instruction for the manufacture of bombs. Herskovitz later told me that Dov had been a sapper in the IDF and that Kahane was particularly inter-ested in Dov's teaching his proteges to make time bombs, which would then be placed in a black community center. "Dov" later disappeared.

JDL members were quick to make use of what they had learned in the camps. They threw Molotov cocktails against blacks in retaliation for the arson of Jewish institutions in Crown Heights in Brooklyn. When firebombs didn't achieve the desired results, they began placing bombs.

At his trial, Kahane did not reveal the whole truth about the JDL summer camps. Rosenthal said bluntly that Kahane was "lying through his teeth." Kahane claimed in court that "We had no idea that it was illegal to explode a bomb on our own property and in a classroom atmosphere." He stated that the bomb had been set off "to graphically illustrate to youngsters of the camp the type of bomb described in pamphlets" of the Black Panthers and Weathermen. Rosenthal responded immediately, "He obviously was lying. That type of bomb was for use."

9

Kahane and the Courts

Hoping to reduce his anticipated sentence, Kahane organized a pressure campaign against Jacob B. Weinstein, the judge at his 1971 trial. Even Kahane's father was mobilized for the campaign. In a letter to the judge, Kahane's father compared his son to the heroes of the Bible and the forefathers of the Jewish people. Articles about the trial began appearing in the *Jewish Press* under different names – one of the heads of the JDL told me that Kahane used about 15 pen names. One of the articles grandiosely maintained that the trial against Kahane and his followers was meant to prepare the way for detente between the U.S. and the USSR, suggesting that if Moscow was successful in its attempts to destroy Kahane, the struggle for Soviet Jewry would suffer a mortal blow. This was Kahane, the master of disinformation, at his peak. What possible connection was there between the struggle for Soviet Jewry and the charges for illegal possession of firearms and explosives?

Kahane ordered his followers to inundate the judge with hundreds of letters. The letters described Kahane as a second Moses or Abraham Lincoln; the victim of a second Dreyfus trial; the Jewish Martin Luther King; a freedom fighter. His brother Nahman went even further; in May 1971, while the trial was in progress, he compared his older brother to giants of the Talmud and Jewish history, calling him the embodiment of Bar

Yohai, Bar- Kochba, Hillel, and Shammai.

Judge Weinstein was not impressed. On July 23, 1971 (seven weeks before Kahane immigrated to Israel), he delivered the sentence: for Kahane – five years' imprisonment (suspended), and a $5,000 fine; Kahane's bodyguard, Chaim Bieber – three years' imprisonment (suspended), and a $2,500 fine. Weinstein unequivocally cautioned Kahane against the use of weapons. "Activities must be carried on without violence," the judge stated. "In this country, at this time, it is not permissible to substitute the bomb for the book as the symbol of Jewish manhood.... These defendants now stand condemned before their fellow citizens as felons – perpetrators of serious crime. For members of Orthodox Jewish families, this is a serious punishment. The court has been informed that Rabbi Kahane wishes to migrate to Israel with his family. He is free to do so."

Before the ink could dry Kahane announced his new motto: "Every Jew a twenty-two."

"I did not ask for mercy," Kahane told the reporters. (Yet Kahane's father had sent the judge a letter begging for clemency.)

Sometimes, there is no other way than violence. Kahane added "I am not against the use of violence if necessary." When Kahane was asked by a reporter who decided upon the use of violence, he replied, "We do" – a patent lie in light of Kahane's highhanded sole rule of the JDL. (As reported in the *New York Times*, July 24, 1971.)

Kahane was quick to violate the conditions of his release. Not only did he tell other Jews to purchase weapons, he himself participated in armed demonstrations. Kahane's probation officer informed the judge of these violations, as well as reports of Kahane's violent speeches to a yeshiva in Williamsburg, urging Jews to acquire firearms for protection. Kahane was summoned by the judge, who warned him that he could be sent to a Federal penitentiary for five years. Kahane, promised Weinstein that he would observe the conditions of his release, not to speak about weapons, nor to visit locations where weapons were present. When Kahane asked the judge about restrictions on his activities in Israel, Weinstein specifically forbade him to encourage the use of weapons in Israel as well. He concluded by advising Kahane to talk to Israelis about other subjects, and expressed his belief that the Israelis didn't need Kahane's encouragement to bear arms. Kahane's failure to comply with the court's order eventually led to his serving time in prison.

By 1975, Kahane was running Kach in Israel and what was left of the JDL in the United States. In January of that year, Kahane and 47 of his followers were arrested during a violent demonstration at the Soviet embassy to the UN. Two shots were fired at the embassy during the course of the demonstration. Such major violations of the terms of his suspended sentence brought Kahane before the court once more. This time, he was ordered to serve the final year of his sentence at the Federal penitentiary in Allenwood, Pennsylvania.

Canada employed an even firmer hand against Kahane when they expelled him in 1976. According to Canadian law, anyone who has been expelled from its territory in the past requires a Canadian visa in order to reenter the country, even if he holds an American passport (normally exempting one from having to request permission to enter the country). In 1972, Kahane threatened to attack a foreign diplomat in Canada. Kahane and six of his followers were expelled. In November 1981, Kahane was arrested in Toronto for illegal entery and was deported from the country. Canadian Immigration Minister John Roberts justified the arrest and expulsion by noting Kahane's illegal activities in the JDL in the United States and in Kach in Israel. Roberts emphasized Kahane's racist incitement in Israel, and his calling for an Israel free of Arabs. Roberts compared Kahane with Hilarion Capucci, the Greek Catholic priest who had been imprisoned by Israel for having smuggled arms into Israel for the PLO. In 1983, Canada refused Kahane entry once again.

England similarly refused Kahane entry. In 1971, Belgium had expelled Kahane after he tried to disrupt proceedings of the World Conference of Jewish Communities on Soviet Jewry in Brussels.

In October 1983, Kahane summed up his role as self- appointed defender of world Jewry: "Let them think of us as thugs. Let them think of us as hoodlums. Let them fear us....

Listen, staying quiet, being nice has never saved one Jew.... Reagan and his people despise Jews. Jews should get out before it's too late" (*Newsday*, October 16, 1983).

10

The JDL and Cultural Exchange

On January 26, 1972, about half a year after Kahane's trial and conviction, the JDL was involved in one of the most tragic events in its short history: the episode leading to the death of a young Jewish woman, Iris Kones.

In January, JDL leaders chose a new target: the offices of the elderly Jewish impresario, Sol Hurok. Hurok had come to America in 1905 from the Ukraine. For half a century he fostered the development of cultural ties with the USSR, arranging concerts, dance, and solo performances by Soviet artists in the U.S. The performances grossed millions of dollars annually, and Hurok was known for the champagne and caviar parties he held for the artists after the theatre. One of America's leading impresarios, Hurok was highly thought of in the Soviet Union, which was interested in increasing cultural ties with the West. His offices were located in a glass skyscraper at the corner of 56th Street and Sixth Avenue in Manhattan.

Hurok was about to complete the preparations for the premier performance of the Osipov balalaika troupe. JDL members often threatened the life of the 83-year-old impresario. They disrupted his productions, setting off smoke bombs and releasing rats during performances by Soviet artists. In their attempts to sabotage the entire American-Soviet cultural exchange, the JDL accused Hurok of insensitivity to the plight of

Soviet Jewry and demanded that he cancel all future tours by Soviet artists.

Hurok refused to bow to JDL pressure. In retaliation, they determined to destroy his offices. On January 26, two young well-dressed men entered Hurok's twelfth-floor office suite and politely asked for the date of a future performance. They were asked to wait for the information, but they quickly left the offices, leaving behind a vinyl-covered briefcase. A time bomb quietly ticked away inside the case. At the same time, two other young men were similarly engaged at a Manhattan location nearby: the offices of Columbia Artists, a film company that also organized visits to the U.S. by Soviet performers.

Before anything could be done, the two bombs exploded. Flames burst forth. The offices were filled with dense, choking smoke. The fire caused great heat. Panic-stricken employees jumped from the windows of the Columbia Artists office, fought their way through the smoke filling the lobby, and escaped to the street. Hurok's office, on a high floor of a skyscraper, encased in hermetically sealed glass, became a deathtrap, filled with lethal smoke. The windows could not be opened. The central air conditioning system spewed forth smoke. Hurok almost choked and was rescued by firefighters; he had to be rushed to the hospital, more dead than alive.

But Iris Kones, a 27-year-old Jewish woman who worked in the accounting department, and two other women with whom she worked tried to escape the smoke. They kept their faces close to the floor, which was covered with wall-to-wall carpeting. The firefighters found them like that when they entered the room, with their faces buried in the carpet and their hair burned. All three were unconscious. Two were successfully resuscitated with the use of oxygen, but Iris had inhaled too much smoke. She died of suffocation. (Twelve other employees were injured; two suffered serious burns.)

At the time of the bombings, Meir Kahane was in Jerusalem. After an anonymous caller telephoned UPI and NBC, chanting the JDL slogan "Never Again!", the UPI correspondent telephoned Kahane for his response. Kahane replied that his people would never commit such an act; only madmen would be capable of it. Zweibon similarly denied JDL complicity in the bombings, suggesting they were provocations by the extreme left who wanted to destroy the JDL's credibility and reputation.

It is more than likely that both Kahane and Zweibon were well aware of the JDL's complicity inthe bombings. By this time, the JDL had split into small underground cells, which enabled them to conceal their actions from the organization's leaders. Yet they continued to receive approval for those actions, either beforehand or afterwards, from the JDL leadership. Fearing that they might be charged with first-degree murder, Zweibon hurriedly cancelled a demonstration against the Osipov balalaika troupe, scheduled for the evening of that same fateful day.

The bombing that resulted in the death of Iris Kones appalled the general public. The rabbi of the temple she had attended referred to it as "bitter fruit of the climate of violence." New York City's Mayor John Lindsay condemned it. Many Jewish leaders wrote to President Nixon, deploring the criminal irresponsibility of the JDL's behavior.

The soviet poet Yevgeny Yevtushenko was in New York at the time. He had been invited to give public readings of his poetry, incluing his famous poem abut the murder of Kiev Jewry during the Holocaust, "Babi Yar." He saw the ruins of Hurok's offices and composed a poem for Iris Kones, Called "Bombs for Balalaikas":

> "Poor Iris,
> Victim of the age,
> You've fallen
> Fragile,
> Dark-eyed
> Jewish girl suffocated by smoke
> As though in a Nazi gas chamber.
> It's hard to vent out poisoned air.
> Damn you, servants of Hell
> Who seek coexistence between peoples
> By building bridges of cadavers."

The police arrested seven people, including three minors, all JDL members. (One of them, Michael Brown, was a planted agent arrested by mistake; he was soon released.) The League responded by picketing police headquarters and charging the chief of police with harassment and anti-Semitism. Those directly responsible for Iris's death, either hid or fled to Israel. The fugitives included Jerome Zeller and several others subpoenaed by the grand jury investigating the crime.

The police nets soon drew in Stuart Cohen, Sheldon Davis, and Sheldon Seigel, three members of the top echelon of the JDL. They were arrested and charged with causing the death of Iris Kones. Kahane hurried back to the United States, and held a press conference at the Belmont Plaza. Kahane charged Nixon with attacking the League. He repeated his denial of JDL complicity in the bombing, and said that the "beautiful Jewish children" taken into custody had been arrested solely because they were JDL leaders.

When the fleeing Jerome Zeller arrived in Israel, he was met by Kahane, who hurried to house him with his brother Nahman, a senior official in the Ministry of Religious Affairs. Zeller later moved to a religious kibbutz, Ma'aleh Hagilboa. One of Kahane's "beautiful children," and a "leader" of the JDL, Zeller was barely 18 years old at the time, and had just begun college.

In March 1973, fourteen months after the death of Iris Kones, the United States requested Zeller's extradition. The Tel Aviv court ordered Zeller's detention in the Abu Kabir prison, where he remained for a month. He was then released on $1,200 bail. By this time, Zeller had been drafted into the Israeli army, serving in the Armored Corps. The extradition proceedings dragged on until the outbreak of the Yom Kippur War. Zeller drove a tank, and was wounded in the battles on Mount Hermon in the Golan Heights. His right hand remained paralyzed as a result of his injuries. The U.S. stopped asking for his extradition. At the time this book was written (1985), Zeller was married with three children. He serves in the IDF reserves on a volunteer basis, since the injuries he sustained in the war exempt him from compulsory reserve duty.

During extradition proceedings in 1973, Kahane was quick to ask whether it was permissible to surrender a Jew to non-Jews. At the end of March 1973, Kahane asked Ovadiah Yosef, then Chief Rabbi of Israel, to issue a ruling prohibiting Israel from surrendering Jews to other countries, citing a passage from Maimonides' *Code*. But who had granted permission to take the life of Iris Kones?

Nor did Kahane stand by his comrades who had been arrested in New York, and did not supply them with legal aid, fearing that he would be implicated in the crime. While the JDL found itself in the most serious legal difficulties in New York, Kahane found every reason to justify his stay in Jerusalem – not the first time he abandoned his people when they were in trouble with the law.

The New York police found five people responsible for placing the bomb in Hurok's office: three were arrested, one fled to Israel, and the fifth person could not be found.

Each of the three JDL members arrested had his own legal counsel. Stuart Cohen was represented by Barry Slotnick, who had once served as go-between for Kanane and Colombo. Bertram Zweibon took on Sheldon David's defense. Sheldon Seigel was represented by Alan M. Dershowitz, who was generally recognized as a lawyer for the left, having defended Angela Davis at one of her trials. Dershowitz, seven years older than Seigel, had grown up in the same neighborhood and attended the same yeshiva before going on to Harvard Law School. Seigel had joined the JDL after an incident on Simchat Torah when Jews were attacked outside their synagogue in Borough Park. A fight developed and there were casualties. Seigel decided to join the JDL so that he could retaliate.

After five months of hearings, the grand jury indicted the three for the murder of Iris Kones.

Dershowitz suspected that his client, Sheldon Seigel, was a police informer. In a confrontation between the two, Seigel suddenly blurted, "I don't work for them. They forced me to give them information. They threatened to kill me if I didn't, and they promised me I would never have to testify against my friends. Now they want me to testify against Cohen and Davis in the Hurok case. I don't want to do that. Can they make me. What can I do?"

Seigel agreed to cooperate with the New York police after he was caught in an amateurish attempt at underground activities typical of the JDL. In April 1971 Seigel initiated a plan to blow up the Manhattan building housing the offices of Amtorg, the Soviet trade delegation. Two bombs were planted. Before they went off, he called the building engineer, told him about the bombs, and chanted the slogan, "Never Again!" The building and the entire area were evacuated. One bomb exploded, but the police succeeded in defusing the second. A special investigating team headed by Santo Parola, quickly discovered that Seigel, masquerading under the name of "Feldman," was responsible. He had purchased the materials neccessary for the construction of the bomb (timers and copper wiring) from an electric-supply store in Borough Park near the League's headquarters. Timers, wires, batteries, and gunpowder were discovered in the trunk of the yellow Volvo that Siegel drove, (registered in his brother Irwin's name). The search was conducted illegally, without prior warning and without a warrant. Seigel and a friend who was with him in the car were arrested, and charged with the possession of explosives. The car was impounded as evidence.

Parola suspected that Seigel was responsible for the bombs in Amtorg, as well as the earlier explosion in Hurok's office. Seigel agreed to serve as a police informer, in exchange for the release of his yellow Volvo, a small enough price for an informer among the ranks of the JDL. Seigel's code name was "Angelo," while Parola was known as "Steve Horowitz." Thanks to the information supplied by Seigel, the local and federal detectives learned of all the JDL's operational plans, were able to stop them ahead of time, and, for all practical purposes, eliminated the JDL.

The first piece of information supplied by Seigel led to the dismantling of a bomb placed by his comrades in the Soviet residence in Glen Cove, Long Island. Seigel later admitted to Parola that he himself had placed the bombs in Amtorg and Glen Cove. He identified those who helped him assemble the bombs, place them, and make the telephone warnings, with the slogan, "Never Again!"

The grand jury met in closed session and heard Seigel's testimony. Indictments were returned against Seigel and six others for the bombs in Amtorg and Glen Cove. In the meantime another serious incident ocurred. A JDL sniper fired into the seventh-floor bedroom of the residence of the Soviet delegate to the UN. Fortunately none of the diplomat's four children asleep in the room were harmed. The sniper fired from the roof of Hunter College, using a Remington 243.

Seigel named the real sniper: Gary Shlian, a 17-year-old. Shlian was arrested while on his way to the airplane which was to take him to Israel.

Seigel told about fantastic plans against Soviet diplomats envisioned by the JDL with the grandiose notion of damaging an emerging detente between the U.S. and the USSR. The first plan had reached the operational stage. JDL members built a radio- controlled model plane, with a wingspan of 6 feet, which could carry 66 sticks of dynamite. The plane could be transported on the top of an automobile and controlled from a distance. JDL members planned to land the plane on top of the Soviet mission to the UN on Park Avenue and explode it.

The second plan concerned dynamiting a Soviet diplomat's car while it was parked in the underground garage of the Soviet Mission. League members conducting surveillance on the diplomat discovered that he parked his car in an accessible location during weekly visits to his mistress. The dynamite would be attached to the bottom of his car at that time, to be detonated by remote control, when the car was later parked in the Soviet Mission's underground garage. Other plans included shelling the Soviet residence in Glen Cove, Long Island and murdering the Soviet ambassador to Washington, Anatoly Dobrynin, as he entered the Soviet embassy.

Acting on Seigel's information, police located the miniature plane in the basement of a house in Borough Park. They also scotched notions of shelling the residence in Glen Cove and assassinating the Soviet ambassador.

Seigel continued working at JDL headquarters in Borough Park, while he was feeding his operator, Parola, a steady stream of information on the League's activities. However, he chose to withhold information on the plan to bomb Hurok's offices. Only after the fatal explosion did Seigel reveal to Parola that it had been he who placed the bomb.

But JDL thugs did succeed in smashing the windows in the New York offices of the Soviet airline, Aeroflot. The Soviets stepped up their pressure on Washington to clamp down on the League. The summit conference, scheduled for the day after the damaging of the Aeroflot office, was cancelled. The Soviets also acted in the cultural sphere. They cancelled the visits to the U.S. of the Bolshoi Ballet and their opera company, which had been arranged by Hurok's office. The JDL's activities continued to irritate the Soviets and embarrass the U.S. The Soviet ambassador to the UN, Yakob Malik, accused the United States of being helpless in dealing with the Zionist hooligans, who he claimed were aggressively preaching the racist ideology of the "Chosen People."

Meanwhile, Dershowitz in a brilliant display of legal tactics, succeeded in having all charges dropped against the three JDL members charged with murder. Dershowitz convinced the court that constitutional rights had been violated, and that Seigel was coerced into becoming an informer. The three went free. Other JDL members who were involved either went into hiding in the U.S. or fled to Israel. The presiding judge, Arnold Bauman, could not bear the defendants' open defiance. He angrily turned to them and asked, "Do you know who isn't in court today? Iris Kones." He added, angrily, "Someone has committed a dastardly, vicious, unforgivable, unforgettable crime...."

Immediately after the trial, Sheldon Seigel and his wife Tova moved to Long Island and opened a furniture factory. In 1980 they moved to Israel, where Sheldon became a contractor. In February 1985, I asked to speak with him, stating that I was writing a book on Kahane. Surprisingly, Seigel replied that he had to receive Kahane's permission for such a meeting. He added that he was not active in Kahane's organizations in Israel. I never received a reply from him. Kahane himself maintained contact with Seigel in Israel, even after Seigel had been exposed as an informer who had turned in his closest asociates. Kahane, who himself cooperated with the authorities in such matters, is not affected by others informing or betraying their comrades.

Zweibon, who had defended Sheldon Davis, told me at the end of 1984 that Sheldon Seigel had placed the bomb. A few days later I met Davis, at a press conference organized by Zweibon and Murry Wilson, now Kahane's enemies. In September 1984 some of Kahane's followers, including two "private detectives," warned Davis to stop bothering Kahane; if not, they would kill him. Davis, who had been executive director of the JDL during the years 1971-73, later studied at the Jewish Theological Seminary. He became a Conservative rabbi, but claims he could not find work because of Kahane's harassment.

Stuart Cohen remained in the United States, and became the director of a travel agency.

Iris Kones's death heralded the death of the Jewish Defense League as a viable organization. Dershowitz believes that the acquittal (or non-conviction, to be more accurate) of the three was instrumental in the League's downfall. Kahane's vocal, hysterical denials of complicity in the wake of Seigel's revelations, made Kahane and the other leaders of the League look like cowards who feared to take responsibility, to show remorse or to ask forgiveness. The Iris Kones affair led to a general demoralization among the ranks of the JDL. Those members who remained in the U.S. after the flight of activists to Israel and Kahane's own immigration opted out of Kahan's dangerous games. Their dreams had been shattered; their idol had feet of clay.

Four factors contributed to the JDL's downfall in the United States: persecution by the authorities, planted agents, the death of Iris Kones, and Sheldon Seigel's betrayal of the organization.

11

Financing Kahane

Meir Kahane is in constant need of large sums of money for his personal affairs. Innocent Jews, who contributed to the Jewish Defense League, never thought that Kahane's honesty and the methods in which he uses their money should be questioned. The JDL-Kach leader was never requested to report on the uses to which this money was put, and no one supervises the way in which Kahane handles money. Despite this blind trust in him, Kahane has never hesitated to use money donated for public causes for his own personal needs, or to use money donated explicitly for one project for another end – all this without the permission of the contributors.

Murry Wilson is a wealthy New Yorker. In the past he was one of the leaders of the JDL, and one of its main contributors. When I met him at the end of 1984 in his New York office, he had become one of Kahane's main enemies. Wilson said that he knew Kahane from 1970, adding in the same breath, "He stole money from us." He told me that in 1972 he gave Kahane $100,000 in cash of his, as well as contributions by four of his friends, for the keymoney purchase of the Zion Hotel in Jerusalem, to serve as a center for JDL activists from the United States. The heads of the JDL, mainly the contributors, wanted to train cadres of young Americans in the former hotel, and then disperse them throughout American college campuses.

They wanted to prepare an elite corps, the future leadership of the League. In April 1972 Kahane purchased the hotel for keymoney, paying the owners $50,000 in cash. The rest of the money, $50,000, was reserved for expenses.

When Wilson visited Israel in July 1972, he was astounded to discover that the center did not fulfill the goals which had been set for it. Although Kahane called the center "Yeshivat Torah Ve'oz" (the "yeshivah of Torah and strength"), the building served neither as a yeshivah nor as a training institute for League activists from the United States. When Wilson returned to America, he gave an oral report to his fellow members of the League's executive board, who were also, at least on paper, the directors of the Zion institute. Wilson discovered that in September 1972, a few months after the purchase of the hotel, Kahane had cancelled the keymoney arrangement with the owners of the building, who paid him more than $50,000 in order to get back their hotel. Kahane used this money to open the offices of the Jewish Defense League in Eretz Israel, in preparation for the Knesset election campaign at the end of 1973, despite his commitment never to run for public office.

Only two members of the JDL executive board, Murry Wilson and Charles Schreiber, voted to take legal action against Kahane for having deceived the contributors. The three other members of the board hesitated, not wanting to "inform" on Kahane to "alien" institutions. They also turned down Wilson and Schreiber's suggestion to summon Kahane to a *din Torah*, a trial by a rabbinical court (an accepted form of mediation among Orthodox Jews), for having misused the money given by Wilson for a specific purpose, and for having taken the money for his own needs. The suggestion was also raised at that board meeting that all five members of the board resign in protest and stop contributing to the League. Wilson did resign from the board in January 1973.

Wilson told me that he had called Kahane a crook on a radio program in New York a few days before I interviewed him; he said that Kahane did not respond to the charge. Wilson stated that Kahane had used contributions for himself, and that he had never given a financial accounting to anyone. Wilson stopped talking, and played for me a cassette with a recording of the radio program. He gave me the cassette, and asked me to take it to Israel and play it for anyone wanting to know the real Kahane.

Wilson estimates the yearly contributions to Kahane, from Americans alone, at "several hundred thousand dollars." He mentioned the name of an accountant who gave Kahane $20,000 during 1984. Wilson provided me with a list of American contributors, listing contributions from $100 to $5,000. He told me that he himself had contributed more than $200,000 in cash for supplies for the JDL camps in the Catskills. Yet, he declared, he and the other contributors did not know that the money which had been intended for activities in the United States had actually been used by Kahane for his purposes in Israel.

A few days after I interviewed Wilson, he held a press conference in the Roosevelt Hotel in Manhattan, where Wilson's restaurant (which he called the world's largest Jewish restaurant) was located. He called the press conference in order to proclaim, with Bertram Zweibon at his side, that Meir Kahane is a "crook." He related that the JDL, except for the fundraising activities directed by Kahane, has been almost inactive after the misuse of funds connected with the Zion Hotel was uncovered. As proof of his charges, Wilson cited Kahane's requesting the JDL leadership to attain money to cover the bills for Meir Schechter's legal work in Israel on behalf of Kahane. These expenses totalled about IL 35,000 (more than $8,000) during the summer of 1974. Most of the items in the detailed bill were for the defense of Kahane's hooligans in Israel who had been arrested for criminal activities, including Kahane's release from jail and the legal work on Kahane's own personal-criminal cases.

Fred Horowitz, Kahane's former neighbor in Laurelton, to whom Kahane still owes $5,000, says that Kahane can be caught on financial matters: he advises giving Kahane a long enough financial rope, and he'll hang himself on it. Horowitz states explicitly that if Kahane is given money to finance the JDL's activities in the United States, he will embezzle it, taking the money for himself. Horowitz adds that Kahane will only "take" the money; he won't steal it, Heaven forbid. He states that Kahane took "thousands of dollars" from him and others in order to smuggle Jews out of the Soviet Union, but actually used the money for himself.

Another contributor stated that he had given Kahane more than $10,000 in cash (so as not to leave any traces) for the establishment of a school in Jerusalem. Instead of the promised school, however, Kahane used the money to help finance his 1973 election campaign. He stated bluntly, "When I got to Jerusalem last year, I found the school was Kahane's campaign headquarters. Let's face it, the man is a fraud" (*New York Post*, October 21, 1974).

A year later, in 1975, Kahane was asked by Shlomo Russ, who was preparing his doctoral thesis on the JDL, where the money missing from the JDL treasury had gone. Kahane, in effect confirming the charges raised by his former contributors, replied that the monies (i. e., contributions) had been used by him (without permission) for his "legal" expenses in Israel. Russ concluded that "in either case, the money was never used for its intended purpose."

Now that Kahane has lost his United States citizenship, and should he lose his appeal on its revocation, he will be forced to apply for a visa each time he wishes to enter the united States. If, as may very well be the case, the United States refuses to grant him an entry visa, Kahane will be effectively cut off from his major sources of funding for all his ventures. Only time will tell whether he can still raise American funds without being physically present at fund-raisers for his activities.

12

Good-bye, New York

When Kahane landed in Lod airport as a new immigrant to Israel, on September 15, 1971, he declared that he would not give up his American citizenship, a promise he kept until the U.S. revoked his citizenship in 1985. He said he would visit America each month to follow the activities of his people there. He also promised that he would not form a political party in Israel, and that he would act to build bridges of understanding between the different elements of Israeli society.

Dr. Joseph Burg, Israel's Minister of the Interior was not happy about issuing Kahane an immigrant's certificate, and was even more reluctant to grant him Israeli citizenship (automatically available for every Jewish immigrant to Israel under the Law of Return). Unlike most Israelis, Burg was aware of Kahane's history. After a year and a half, Burg grudgingly granted Kahane citizenship to avoid battle initiated by Kahane in 1972.

In a speech he delivered before a military court in Ramalleh in 1980 Kahane declared "I left the exile to live in the Land of Israel, not because I fled persecution, but because I knew what the *mitzvah* [commandment] of Zionism is." In his book *Time to Go Home*, Kahane was sharply critical of Jews who dutifully recite "Next year in Jerusalem" in their prayers, but who intend to remain in the exile.

75

The truth, of course is that Kahane did not immigrate to Israel out of Zionist motives, but only after Judge Weinstein gave him a five-year suspended sentence, effectively ending Kahane's political activity in America. There was also a second reason for his immigration. His wife and four children had preceded him to Jerusalem, hoping that he would not be quick to follow them. Libby's father, Ya'akov Blum, told a reporter that his daughter had been unhappy in New York because of her husband Meir's infidelities. He said his daughter was "a beaten woman," who feared for her children's safety in the United States because of her husband's miltant actions. She grieved when her 12-year-old son was arrested at a demonstration at the Soviet Embassy in Washington; Meir was pleased. In Israel, none of their children participate in their father's actions. Zweibon told me that Libby would not leave Meir because of her religious belief. JDL activists in the U.S. stated that Kahane expressed his willingness at one time to divorce Libby, who had left for Israel. One of Kahane's closest advisors confirmed that the two had considered divorce, but were finally reconciled. In Jerusalem, Libby, a librarian, watches from the side lines, taking no part in her husband's activities, and offering him no support.

Kahane had made an earlier attempt to settle in Israel. He came to the country in 1962, the same year his brother Nahman immigrated to Israel. On the eve of his depature, Kahane promised his family that he would "soon" be a member of the Israeli government. His uncle, Isaac Trainin, recalls that Kahane hoped David Ben-Gurion would come to the airport to greet him upon his arrival. He wanted to head the department for international relations at Bar Ilan University, but his dream was not fulfilled. He wrote to his parents that he was very excited by a meeting he had with the two Chief Rabbis in Israel. He spent several months in a religious kibbutz, where he wanted to be accepted as rabbi, on a trial basis, but the kibbutz members refused because of his heavy stutter and because they were not especially excited about his personality. His mother recalled that he was very upset upon his return to the U.S. and claimed that he returned because of "all the fighting among Jewish factions in

Israel." His brother Nahman did not conceal the truth; he stated that Meir was not absorbed into Israeli society because of personal reasons. Trainin wanted to help Kahane find a job as a teacher in the Hawthorne school, but Kahane was rejected because of his strict Orthodox views. Trainin feels that the Jewish community bears certaim responsibility for Kahane's later radical views and the establishment of the JDL because of its rejection of him in the early 1960's.

A month after arriving in Israel in 1971, Kahane opened an office in Jerusalem and appointed Meir Schechter as the legal counsel of the Jewish Defense League in Israel. Formal activities, including the registration of the League as a nonprofit organization, started in 1972. A four-page statement of principles was written for this purpose. It said nothing about expelling Arabs from the country.

The statement of principles declared, rather, that the League had been established in order "to inculcate the concept of 'love of one's fellow Jew' among the Jewish people." It vowed "to renew the image of the Jew of yesterday, the Jew who treads on the soil of Israel with pride, head held high, the Jew who refuses to compromise about his Jewishness. Specifically in these days, we shall raise the banner of the eternal slogan, 'Never Again'."

Another passage averred "that since the Land of Israel is not Brooklyn, and violence is out of place here, the League must be viewed as an educational body, which aspires to emphasize the Jewish nature and feeling in every sphere of our lives." The ink was hardly dry on the document before Kahane led his hooligans in the same violent tactics he had used in Brooklyn.

Yet another statement declared the League a nonpolitical body, "...the League will not turn into a political party." Kahane stated in an interview in January 1972 that his running for the Knesset "would ruin the League." One year later, Kahane ran in elections for the Knesset. When a reporter asked why, given his recent promises, Kahane said he was in the race "because of the government's desire to eliminate the League; a member of Knesset, however, cannot be eliminated. A vision cannot be realized without power, and power comes with a party." After his election to the Knesset in 1984, Kahane promised his followers that he would be Defense Minister within a few years.

The sixth principle in the League statement promised that "as an organization, which unites within itself the widest spectrum of opinions and views, the League will act to draw closer the various groups, such as the religious and nonreligious, Ashkenazim and Oriental Jews... We will serve as a bridge between the various groups." In fact, the League in Israel and Kach are racist movements, preaching hatred and division between religious and secular Jews, between Ashkenazi and Sephardi Jews, and between Jew and Arab. Most of Kahane's followers are Sephardic Jews, whom he incites against both Arabs and Ashkenazi Jews.

13

Kahane in Israel

Within a year after settling in Israel, Kahane violated the conditions of his suspended sentence in the U.S. by initiating a plot to smuggle arms abroad. In August 1972, three JDL leaders in Israel – Meir Kahane, Avraham Herskovitz, and Yossi Shneider – embroiled Amihai Paglin in an attempt to smuggle arms from Israel to the JDL in New York. Paglin, head of operations in the pre-1948 Irgun Tzva'i Leumi, was a lecturer at JDL seminars in Jerusalem. According to Herskovitz, Paglin had private caches of arms that had been captured by the IDF in the 1956 and 1967 wars.

When eleven Israeli athletes were murdered by Palestinian terrorists on September 5, 1972 during the Munich Olympics, the arms-smuggling conspiracy took on international dimensions to "avenge" the murder of the Israelis. According to Herskovitz, Kahane had received information – presumably leaked by Israeli security services – that the weapons used by the Black September terrorists in Munich had been sent to them via the Libyan embassy in Rome. The Libyan embassy was now targeted for attack in the folowing fantastic scenario outlined by Herskovitz: fifteen JDL members, some from Israel but most from the United States, would be dispatched to Rome to "take over" the Libyan embassy. After sending the arms from Israel, Herskovitz would proceed to Europe to participate in diversionary tactics. A female member of the JDL strike force, feigning advanced pregnancy, would appear at the entrance of the Libyan embassy in Rome, shouting:

"What did that Libyan do to me? He got me pregnant and then threw me out!"

In the ensuing confusion, the JDL force would enter the embassy, kill half its staff and hold the other half hostage while negotiating a return flight to Israel.

Why the mass murder?

"So that they would know immediately that we were serious," says Herskovitz, "and to gain headlines and publicity in the Arab world." Remaining staff members would be forced to lie beside their murdered associates, "so that they would later say it was not worthwhile to get involved with madmen like us." If demands for a safe passage to Israel, accompanied by the Israeli ambassador in Rome, were not met, the remaining staff members would be periodically killed. All the attackers, as well as the members of the Libyan embassy, were to be equipped with M-16 rifles, bulletproof vests, and raincoats to conceal the vests, so that it would be impossible to tell Libyan from Jew during the departure from the embassy. The Libyans' rifles, of course, would not be loaded.

In preparation for the attack, Herskowitz visited Paglin at his factory in Petah Tikvah to coordinate arrangements for smuggling out arms. At a prearranged time and place on September 13, Herskovitz and Yossi Shneider presumably received a crate from Paglin containing the following weapons: the barrel of a Karl Gustav submachine gun; the body of a Karl Gustav and a collapsible stock, bearing a number in Arabic; two magazines with bullets; the body of a Karl Gustav, with the inscription "Port Said Egypt" in Arabic on its stock, the barrel and a cloth shoulder strap; two magazines, wrapped in a copy of an Israeli newspaper from October 3, 1971; a 9 mm. Baretta pistol, two loaded magazines and a cloth holster (IDF ammunition); a short Baretta, loaded with an empty magazine, a full magazine, and a box of 9 mm. bullets; three Israeli Mills grenades, without fuses; two boxes of 9 mm. bullets; a box of 25 bullets of Egyptian manufacture; a box of 50 9 mm. bullets; a nylon bag with 50 9

80

mm. bullets; a paper bag with 100 9 mm. bullets.

Close to the 13th of September, Paglin gave Kahane and Shneider three fuses for the Mills grenades. When Herskovitz received the weapons from Paglin, he also received a bill from the "Israel Food Machinery Company."

Had he known what was in the crate?, I asked Herskovitz during our interview.

"Not exactly," he hedged. A bill of lading from the Israel Food Machinery Company listed the contents of the crate as a roller, priced at $46, for the manufacture of biscuits. Herskovitz and Shneider brought the crate to a shipping agent in Tel Aviv, paid the shipping costs, informing the agency's inquisitive clerk that the package contained the biscuit roller listed in its bill of lading.

On September 13, the crate arrived at El Al's freight department in Lod airport, where it was held when suspicions were raised about its contents. Herskovitz was arrested 24 hours later and taken by the police to Lod to open the package. He reiterated that it contained equipment for baking biscuits and denied knowledge of any other contents. When the package was finally opened, Herskovitz recalls, "I looked surprised. Actually, I was surprised to see a Karl Gustav in it. I thought that they had packed an Uzi."

He claims that Kahane informed on him and Shneider, that the police knew abut the whole plan beforehand and had even shown him photographs of his and Shneider's meeting with Paglin in Petah Tikvah.

Before he himself was arrested on October 1, Kahane told a reporter from the *New York Times* that although the operation had been frustrated by Israel's security services the publicity surrounding it was worth a million dollars.

Yossi Shneider, "political commander" of the aborted operation, was suspected by the police, along with four accomplices, of receiving the arms from IDF soldiers and passing them along to Paglin. During their investigation, the police learned that Paglin's role was limited to packing the weapons in his factory. Shneider told me Kahane had planned the entire operation, and that Kahane had made the first contact with Paglin. When I asked Shneider if Kahane had really informed on Paglin to the security services, merely in order to win headlines, he replied cautiously, "There was a rumor that Kahane wanted to make a deal with the authorities". But Shmuel Tamir, Paglin's lawyer, repeatedly charged that Kahane had turned in the entire group.

Throughout the trial, Tamir reiterated that charge, suggesting in addition that Kahane's openly provocative acts in Israel were intended to concretely demonstrate that Israel was incapable of ruling the administered territories or of protecting the holy places in Jerusalem. He further described Kahane as a rabble-rouser and provocateur who wanted to evict Israel's Arabs.

Paglin served twice under Menahem Begin, first in the pre-1948 underground Irgun Tzva'i Leumi as Begin's chief of operations, and in the late 1970's as advisor on terrorism to the then Prime Minister. On March 1, 1985, I asked Begin whether Kahane had embroiled Paglin in the affair. Begin's reply was an unequivocal "Yes, certainly. The episode is well-known. I learnt about it after the fact."

Israeli press coverage on Kahane during that period was quite sympathetic. Even the presiding judge at the trial, Hadassah Ben-Ito, a highly intelligent judge, took the defendant's presumed good intentions into account. She stated in her verdict, on November 17, 1974, "No one argues that these defendants are criminals who wanted to benefit, or who tried to attain personal gains from these acts. The opposite is true. We are dealing with people who are willing to endanger themselves, to cause suffering to themselves and their families; all this for the aim of the public good. The goal or goals of the defendants – not only those enumerated in the bylaws of their association, but also those which are known in public and which were mentioned during this trial – are legal aims, and at least part of them are accepted by the public. I refer especially to their stubborn fight to cause permission to immigrate for Russian Jewry, and their desire to find ways to war against Arab terrorism. They certainly should not be punished for these goals, nor for their devoting their lives to work for the public good."

Ben-Ito gave Kahane and Herskovitz suspended sentences of two years imprisonment, and Shneider and Paglin one-year suspended sentences.

14

Kahane and Population Exchange

Criminal charges against Kahane made headlines throughout 1973, the year he first decided to run for the Knesset. Three cases stood out: the arms smuggling attempt in September 1972, conspiracy to assassinate foreign diplomats (such as Brezhnev on his visit to the U.S.), and the charge of "incitement to rebellion" levelled against Kahane by the Israeli government for urging the emigration of Arabs from Israel.

While trying to clear himself of arms smuggling charges in late September, Kahane refrained from making strong statements about moving Arabs out of the country. Indeed, a newspaper interview published at the time quotes him as saying: "I'm not willing to evict even one Arab, but it's necessary to stop playing games with them. We are not willing to give them full rights, and we're not willing to have them become a majority."

Yet only two months later, once he received his suspended sentence for attempted arms smuggling – Kahane launched his letter-writing campaign, urging Arabs to emigrate from Israel. To that end, he enlisted the support of Emanuel Naji Huri, a Christian Arab from the upper Galilee village of Pasota. Huri describes himself as having worked with the pre-state Haganah and with "various bodies and institutions" (hinting at his involvement with Israeli secret services). He points with pride to letters of commendation from the Prime Minister's office for his "services to the state."

Kahane bestowed the grandiose title of "National Coordinator of the Emigration Fund of the Jewish Defense League" on Huri and set about sending out letters to the Arab citizens of Israel. The letters, mailed in December 1972 and January 1973, presumed to speak in the name of "Citizens of the Jewish State", and were addressed to "the Arabs of Hebron, Nablus, Ramleh, etc." The text read:

"It is clear that the citizens of the Jewish state will never agree to surrender Eretz Israel [the Land of Israel] or to partition it and dismember it. There is no possibility of a retreat from the territories of Eretz Israel which were liberated in 1967. This being the case, and since we respect the Arab national sentiment, we realize that a condition of perpetual tension is liable to be created between the Jewish majority and the Arab minority, as in Northern Ireland. It is desirable, for tranquillity and fraternity, to take steps, ahead of time, to prevent this danger. It is desirable that each people live in its own state, and not under the rule of another people. We therefore appeal to you, and propose that you emigrate from Eretz Israel. We are therefore establishing the 'Emigration Fund,' which will assist every Arab willing to leave the country. If you are willing to emigrate, we turn to you and ask that you inform us of:

1) the number of people in your family, so that we can work out a plan to pay each family, in accordance with its size;

2) if you are willing to sell your apartment to a Jew, and if so, when;

3) to which country you would prefer to immigrate. Please inform us of your order of priorities.

Please inform us of these details by return mail, and as soon as possible.

Sincerely yours,
The Jewish Defense League in Eretz Israel
P. O. B. 7287 Jerusalem"

On February 24, 1973, *El Fajr*, an Arab newspaper published

84

in East Jerusalem, sharply criticized Kahane's transfer plan, referring to him as a "mass murderer, criminal, the devil Kahane." Publishing a list of those who presumably wanted to emigrate under Kahane's plan, the paper set up a fund, financed by Palestinians, to pay for the "mass murderer's" emigration abroad. They collected IL2000 (about $500).

On March 1, Kahane called a press conference in Tel Aviv to introduce yet another player in his drama of migration. Dr. William Perl, a Washington, D.C. psychologist and JDL leader in America, had established the "Committee for the Immigration of Arabs from Israel" in the United States. According to Perl, a corporation with shares had been set up, through which necessary funds could be raised for the migration of "hundreds of thousands of Arabs."

Like Paglin, William Perl was another figure with a distinguished record, who had been taken in by Kahane. Born in Prague, Perl and his family moved to Vienna when he was six. As joint chairman of the Revisionist Zionist organization in Vienna in 1939, Perl was given the task of arranging the transfer of European Jews to mandatory Palestine in conjunction with the Irgun Tzva'i Leumi's "illegal immigration" operation. After Germany annexed Austria, it was Perl who raised the idea of obtaining Nazi assistance for the emigration of European Jews, arguing that it would benefit both sides: the Jews would be able to go to Palestine; the Nazis would further their goal of freeing Europe of Jews.

Toward those ends, Perl called on Adolf Eichmann. After humiliating Perl and demanding written proposals, Eichmann summarily rejected the plan. But Perl did not give up. He went to Berlin to protest Eichmann's decision and returned to Vienna with emigration permission for an additional 5000 Jews. (Perl estimated that he was successful in saving 18,000 Jews).

At the press conference in Tel Aviv, Perl told reporters that committees for Arab migration from Israel had been set up in Los Angeles and Washington and were in the process of formation in Miami and San Diego. Their plan called for selling shares at $2 each in a corporation named "New Horizons" that had been established for the project. The funds raised were to be offered to Arabs, the potential emigrants, in payment for their houses and lands at a higher price than market value. Jewish investors could then be attracted to the locations vacated by Arabs. Thus, Perl explained, both sides would be satisfied.

But Perl and Kahane were pushing a pipe dream. Once requests for information came in from some naive Arabs, it became clear that there was no operative plan for emigration, nor was there any corporation for raising funds. (Three years later, Perl was tried and convicted for conspiring to shoot two Soviet diplomats in Washington.)

During the height of his publicity campaign in mid-March, Kahane was invited to Emanuel Naji Huri's village home for a meeting with six families of Arab notables. "My plan is based on care for the state and the Jewish people on the one hand," Kahane told his hosts, "and on care for the Arab people living here, on the other. I don't want our children to continue to be estranged. This is the land of the Jewish people and you will never be more than a minority here. The time has come to speak the truth, to suggest you emigrate willingly and not as a result of compulsion, heaven forbid. I don't want us to become a second Cyprus or Ireland."

That same month at a Jewish town, Kahane warned that there would soon be an Arab majority in Israel because of their high birth rate, leading to an Arab takeover of the country through democratic means.

Kahane's growing aversion to democracy in Israel, as well as the real intent behind his plans for Arab emigration, is disclosed in an interview he later granted the *Los Angeles Herald Examiner*. In a 1981 article, titled *Portrait of a Zealot*, Gary Rosenblatt reports that Kahane's basic platform for solving Israel's problems is to deport the country's Arabs – by force, if necessary. "I'd go to the Arabs and tell them to leave... I'd promise generous compensation. If they refused, I'd forcibly move them out." Would he do this with midnight deportations in cattle cars? Kahane was asked. "Yes," he answered, adding: "I'm not a racist. A racist is a Jew who says Arabs can be equal citizens in a Jewish state." According to his calculations, Arabs would constitute a majority in Israel by the year 2006.

In the course of Kahane's letter-writing campaign early in 1973, Kahane was called upon to attend yet another kind of meeting with an Israeli minority after letters were "mistakenly" sent to Druze soldiers serving in the Israeli army. There was a need for an immediate *sulcha*, a reconciliation meeting. Kahane feared Druze retaliation. The meeting was set up in Haifa by Druze sheikh Hatam Halabi, together with Druze leader Jabber Mu'adi. Kahane arrived at the meeting with Shimeon Rahamin, author of the first letter, and with Yoel Lerner. Kahane begged the Druze forgiveness, emphasizing that a mistake had been made and that the letter had never been intended for the Druze.

Fifty Druze attended the meeting. They spoke of eternal friendship between the Jews and Druze of Israel. At one point a Druze lecturer at Haifa University rose to announce: "The Druze identify with the Arabs." He was immediately silenced.

According to Rahamin, Sheikh Halabi wanted to join the League, but Kahane explained that League membership was composed entirely of Jews. Halabi reputedly had to make do with voluntary activity for Kach during its 1973 election campaign.

At the beginning of April 1973, Emanuel Huri, National Coordinator of the Emigration Fund, prepared to leave for the United States on a JDL-funded mission, to stress the importance of the Fund "from the viewpoint of an Israeli Arab," and to raise money. The Ministry of Interior delayed issuing Huri's passport. Initially, it claimed doubts about his citizenship, followed by reports that his departure was opposed by the police because Huri was involved in a criminal trial. After Israeli opposition was overcome, the American Consulate in Israel refused Huri an American visa.

On April 20, 1973, Jerusalem's district attorney issued a charge sheet against Meir Kahane, JDL chairman, and against Yoel Lerner, a member of the organization's secretariat. Charges cited the letters sent by the group, urging Arab emigration, as "incitement to rebellion," designed to arouse and inflame relationships between the various groups living in the state, to encourage a lack of unity amongst themselves, and to exacerbate feelings of bad will and hostility among the various segments of population in the country.

Huri claims that the government's speedy response to outbursts of anger in the Arab sector was responsible for Arabs' changing their minds about emigration, leading to the shelving of the JDL's plan. In the end, Kahane received lots of publicity but no Arab emigrants. Before he publicized his program, approximately 400 Arabs emigrated annually; after the publication of his program, the number dropped to 120. Yet Huri was quick to defend him after Kahane was indicted. "A very honest Jew, a bit nervous perhaps, but smart as the devil," said Huri. "There is no need to punish him because of the letters. The government claims the letters hurt Arabs' feelings. That is not correct, in my opinion. Many Arabs want to emigrate so that they won't be dragged into a conflict between their loyalty to Israel and their national identification." Those who knew Huri maintained he was using Kahane for his own purposes; Huri, himself, declared that if he had enough money, he would emigrate from Israel. In the end, Huri was forced to leave the country for Australia because of threats on his life.

Kahane was represented at his trial by Aaron Papo. Papo disclosed the line of defense he intended to employ during the trial. It turned out to be effective. He maintained that Kahane's letter to the Arabs was a legitimate appeal for a peaceful transfer of population. If Kahane had violated the law, argued Papo, then so had leading Zionists who had preceded him.

Papo intended to introduce the speeches and writings of leading Zionists and leaders of Israel who had advocated removing the Arabs by one method or another. Three weeks after the establishment of the State of Israel, Papo pointed out that Moshe Sharett, the leading dove in Ben-Gurion's cabinet, called the flight of Arabs from the country "one of the most impressive events of our generation." The concept of transfers of population were also supported, Papo maintained, by Chaim Weizmann, head of the Zionist Federation, Revisionist leader Ze'ev Jabotinsky, Berl Katzenelson, one of Mapai's outstanding members, Yitzhak Tebenkin, head of the Kibbutz Meuhad, and others. Katzenelson wrote, "My conscience is entirely clear on this. A distant neighbor is better than a close enemy. They will not lose by their transfer, and we certainly not."

Kahane's offering money (which he did not have) to the Arabs so that they would emigrate was simply a rehash of the plan formulated by John Philby, an Englishman who had converted to Islam. Philby's plan called for an Arab federation headed by Ibn Saud. For a payment of twenty million pounds sterling, Ibn Saud would absorb all the Arabs of Palestine within his realm, and the Jews would receive a land free of Arabs. According to Papo, this proposal was supported by Moshe Shertok (later Sharett), "foreign minister" of the Jewish state in the making, by Golda Meirson (later Meir), and by David Ben-Gurion. In 1937, when the British Peel Commission proposed partitioning Mandatory Palestine into two countries, they recommended encouraging Arab emigration by all means, including compulsion, from the areas intended for the Jewish state.

Papo said that Golda Meir used to tell her associates she was afraid to get up every morning and hear that another Arab had been born in Israel. (This was later confirmed for me by one of Mrs. Meir's spokesmen from that period – Y.K.)

Less than a year before Kahane sent his letters, Eliezer Livneh, a leader of the Greater Israel movement, had called for the transfer of Arabs from Israel in an article published in Ha'aretz. A month after Kahane and Lerner were indicted, Livneh argued (in the Greater Israel journal) that Kahane's ideas were a direct outcome of Foreign Minister Abba Eban's plea for the return of Judea and Samaria because of the presence of a large Arab population in those areas.

Papo says he learned that corporations for Arab emigration had been founded during Levi Eshkol's term as Prime Minister. Papo intended to question government ministers on this. Clearly, Papo intended to turn the trial into a public forum. The trial began on May 21, 1973, and continued, with long breaks, until May 5, 1975.

Midwar through the trial, on December 6, 1974, Dr. Aaron Davidi, former head of the Paratroop Corps, was interviewed in the newspaper, *Ma'ariv*. Davidi's statements further served Papo's line of defense. When asked how he would solve the

Palestinian problem, Davidi replied, "In the simplest and most humane manner – the transfer of all the Palestinians from their present locations to the Arab lands." When the interviewer said that the Arabs would not want such a solution, Davidi stated, "They will. This is very important for both the Jews and the Arabs. They will accept it, if they have no choice. The Arab states are spread out over a territory of more than ten million square kilometers. The density of the Arabs is the lowest in the world. Would it be a problem to absorb one milion there, and to arrange housing and employment for them, with the help of the great wealth?" About the possibility of transferring Arabs to Jordan where they could establish a Palestinian state, Davidi asserted, "Let them establish whatever they want there. Is it the task of the State of Israel to establish a state for them? The Jewish people has only one task: to build, to make bloom, to develop, to improve the State of Israel and protect it. It's enough for us to carry out this task."

Throughout the legal proceedings Papo argued that the law under which Kahane had been charged was a hangover from the colonial period, derived from Mandatory ordinance against disturbing public order. He also cited other instances of population transfer, such as the work of Fridtjof Nansen, who won a Nobel Peace Prize for transferring Turks and Bulgarians to their respective countries before World War I, the transfer of more than a million Turks and several hundred thousand Greeks after the war, the mass transfers of population following World War II, and the tens of millions of Moslems and Hindus moved between India and Pakistan. All the peoples had been absorbed in their new homes, unlike the Palestinians, who had been kept for decades by the Arab countries as "refugees" in temporary camps that spawned hatred and terror directed against Israel.

Papo called on the prosecutor and district attorney. He asked them to withdraw the charge of incitement to rebellion, terming it "madness." He argued that they were taking a colonial law, such as the British had used to resolve ethnic quarrels in India, Palestine and their other colonies, and applying it to political beliefs in modern day Israel. Papo threatened to prove in court that Kahane was only repeating statements that had been made by leading Zionists and Israeli government officials, as well as prominent non-Jews, favoring the transfer of Arabs. He added that he could show letters from Arabs, accepting Kahane's proposals.

Michael Kirsh, district attorney at the time, heard Papo out, but did not respond. Papo believes that the prosecution feared confrontation with the defense in court. After the conversation with Kirsh, Papo received a notice that the continuation of the trial had been postponed. It has not been resumed to this day.

Kirsh, today the head of a legal firm in Israel, denies that he might have been convinced by Papo's arguments. "I don't remember the conversation with Papo," he told me when I spoke with him in 1985.

Uzi Hason, prosecutor for the case, had a better memory: "As best I can recall, the trial was postponed. After you called me, I reconstructed the episode, together with Kirsh, who agreed. According to procedure, I placed an announcement of postponement in the file; it was the court which was supposed to have notified the defense attorney. Clearly, there was a postponement; it is also correct that Papo did not request one." Hason added that the postponement may have been decided upon because the testimony of one of their witnesses did not meet the prosecution's expectations and because two of their Arab witnesses failed to appear at the trial. When I asked, Hason told me that the file of the case had been burned. (Israeli law permits the burning of files after seven years.)

Papo expresses amazement at what Kirsh and Hason said. Given the fact that neither Papo nor Meir Schechter, Lerner's lawyer, requested a postponement, the vague way in which the trial was effectively ended, and the indirect manner in which the defense learned of the postponement, Papo suggests that the prosecutor and district attorney were persuaded by his arguments, despite what they say.

Yossi Dayan, former Kach secretary-general, claims he and Kahane contacted Moshe Sharon (Menachem Begin's advisor on Arab affairs during 1977-78) for advice on handling the 7000 responses from Arabs that the movement presumably received. According to Dayan:

"Professor Sharon conceived of the idea of forming dummy enterprises in Latin America, to settle those agreeing to emigrate," and Sharon "advised us to operate through the Mossad, but he resigned from his post a few weeks later."

When I asked Moshe Sharon for his response, he was shocked by Dayan's statements. "A fairy tale. Nonsense. This is totally opposed to my philosophy." Sharon added that Huri "appeared to me to be disturbed.... Huri used Kahane in order to go abroad. He had a screw missing, as is the case with all of Kahane's people. He was a flatterer and constant informer in the military government, which once was located in Tarshiha." Speaking of the "program," and the advice he presumably gave Dayan and Kahane, Sharon said, "Kahane and Dayan used to speak with me on occasion. I listened to them. Afterwards I had to calm the Arab population.... Kahane's people fabricate all kinds of stories about people and defame them.... If you listened to them, and didn't respond, they were quick to leave you with a 'program' in their hands which they attributed to the person with whom they had spoken. They involved people. Afterwards they would publicize that they had not only spoken with a certain person, but that they also had programs. Kahane spoke with me once on the telephone about his usual nonsense concerning the emigration of the Arabs. I then had a problem to prove to the Arabs that we, the government of Israel, had no dealings with this madman. Yossi Dayan is a nuisance. He nags. He calls on the telephone. They write the names of many people in their telephone book, and then claim that they have agents in the government. Kahane spits out the names of VIP's. He's a name-dropper. I told the Arab leadership that we don't have any conection with this madman Kahane. The whole topic of emigration and the letters to the Arabs was a gimmick, a scheme, for personal publicity. Kahane and his people are a band of madmen who enjoy their actions, because they don't have anything else in their lives."

15

Letters from a Friend

A few months after being indicted for "inciting to rebellion," Kahane faced yet another charge. He was apprehended for sending letters from Jerusalem to his cohorts in the U.S., outlining a criminal conspiracy with international implications. (A total of four letters were sent, on the 17th and 24th of May, and the 12th of June, 1973.) The indictment against Kahane in the Jerusalem District Court mentioned four major crimes which were being planned: the murder of citizens of foreign states; the kidnapping of citizens of foreign states; the bombing and shooting into foreign embassies; the placing of bombs in buildings in which American corporations conduct economic activity, both inside and outside the United States. All of this, of course, clearly violated the conditions of Kahane's suspended sentence.

Presented in court on June 29, 1973, by State Attorney Gabriel Bach, the indictment declared that Kahane's attempt to form a conspiracy against the United States could harm Israel's relationship with the United States, a country friendly to Israel. (Eleven years later, Bach served as chairman of the Central Elections Commission, and ruled to invalidate Kach from running in the general election held that year; his decision was overturned by the High Court of Justice.) The trial opened on March 11, 1974, before Judge Ya'akov Bazak.

The letters that Kahane sent to addresses in the United States never reached their destinations. They were intercepted by the military censor before they left Israel. A telegram did leave the country. The first letter, dated May 17, was addressed to Aliza Greenblum, who was requested to pass the letter along to "Josh" (who today lives in the Etzion Bloc in Israel). A copy of an article from the *Jerusalem Post* of May 17, 1973 was included with the letter. The article conjectured that the Kashkosh family in Baghdad had been murdered by the Iraqis in response to the IDF raid on Beirut. Kahane demanded a reprisal by remote control: "If we can't find some Jew(s) willing to blow up the Iraqi embassy in Washington ... and if we can't get someone to shoot a Russian diplomat (anyone) we are Jewish pigs and deserve what we get."

In the second letter addressed to Shalom Klass, publisher of the *Jewish Press* Kahane requested that the newspaper print an enclosed article, which described the deplorable state of Iraqi Jewry, and which spoke of the urgent need to increase activities on behalf of Soviet Jewry. Kahane expressed his disappointment with the actions that had been taken until then by Jewish organizations in the United States; he stated that parades and demonstrations would not be effective, and called for immediate violent action. He described in detail what he wanted: Brezhnev's visit to the United States must fail, so that the Russians would not succeed in achieving detente with the U.S. unless they took steps for the welfare and immigration to Israel of Soviet Jews. "Where are the Jews who will strike now immediately at a Soviet diplomat, causing Brezhnev to cancel his trip to the United States and thus stop the detente that will decimate Soviet Jewry?" Kahane wrote.

In the letter to Aliza Greenblum Kahane also reiterated "All possible efforts have to be made to stop Brezhnev's trip or, failing that, to ruin it. At the same time immediate action must be taken against the Iraqis and Syrians before more Jews are murdered. I suggest:

1) An immediate kidnapping and/or shooting of a Soviet diplomat. I once received the name of Alexander Ereskovski, 4513 31st Street, Shirlington, Va. Apt. 101. He drove a 1965

Chevrolet DPL 2317. A careful check should be made to see if this information is still pertinent. A very discreet and careful visit to Dr. William Perl, 8411 48th Avenue, College Park, MD Md. (sic) will help.

2) A very QUICK request by a high school group for a Soviet speaker to explain the Russian side of the argument can be made. If done NOW by a high school student in JDL (I suggest Mara) you will know exactly when and where the Russian will be.

3) A bomb at the offices of Occidental Petroleum to warn Armand Hammer and any other people against deals with the Russians. Similarly, at a Chase Manhattan Bank since David Rockefeller opened a bank in Moscow

4) Take over a house at the back of the Soviet Embassy in Washington and fire shots into it; or the AFL building roof across the street from the front of it.

5) A building in Washingtonwas (sic) used by the Iraqis as their Embassy before they broke off diplomatic relations. Perl knows where it is. It is still officially theirs and an explosion there would be excelent (sic).

6) If three actions could be done at the same time, i. e. Occidental, Chase and a Russian; or an Iraqi, Occidental and a Russian it would be excellent but the main thing is that something must be done. I suggest that concentration on a Russian in his house and the Iraqi building (and if possible, Occidental).

This is urgent for the survival of these Jews or else I would never ask you to risk things.

After everything is done wait to hear the news broadcasts and if no innocent person is killed, phone the press."

The telegram, which was sent to the JDL in New York, read, "Urgent Do whatever necessary cancel or ruin Brezhnev visit and act on Iraqi Jews Both vital to Jewish survival Repeat do whatever neccesary

JDL Executive Board

Jerusalem"

Kahane was arrested and kept in detention for a month, before he was released on bail. He tried to smuggle letters to the U.S. from jail. One, the fourth and last, was addressed to Jean

Linger, who was asked to pass it along to Ari Ilowitz. Again, Kahane urged committing acts of terrorism, seizing and taking control of the offices of the International Red Cross or of a Soviet office. "Do whatever you think is necessary to smash détente."

After Kahane was arrested, his American passport was taken from him. His followers, Yossi Shneider and Shimeon Rahamin, ran to Menahem Begin, then head of the opposition in the Knesset. They asked him to use his influence and connections to have Kahane released from jail. Rahamim could remember in 1985 only that Begin gave an evasive answer. Shneider, however, could still quote Begin's reply: "If Kahane writes letters in such an open manner, what do you want from me?"

Kahane was desperate. He was in urgent need of money. He had made preparations to run for the Knesset in the 1973 elections, the year in which he was tried for three crimes (arms smuggling, conspiracy to murder foreign diplomats and wreck the Brezhnev visit, and incitement to rebellion). These events were planned so that his name would not be out of the headlines for even one day during the campaign. Incarceration in prison upset Kahane's plans to raise money in the United States. Kahane was now totally dependent upon one of his contributors, Hilton Kramer. Kramer, a New Jersey lawyer, had committed himself to raise funds for Kahane's electoral campaign. Kahane's letters to him grew more desperate. He "urgently" requested $13,000. Kramer replied that the Messiah would have to appear to raise the sums of money Kahane wanted. Kahane could leave Israel only after the conclusion of the trial on June 28, 1974, when Judge Bazak gave him a two-year suspended sentence.

An analysis suggests that Kahane sent the letters and telegram in an intentionally open manner so that the censor and the security services would stop his orders to kill, and so that they would be publicized by the media. He hoped to win headlines to help his electoral campaign, emphasizing his role on behalf of Soviet Jewry.

In his verdict Justice Bazak stated, "It is possible, of course, to doubt the degree of seriousness of such an immature plan of bombs and terrorist acts sent by regular mail, without using any form of code, and not even allusions, but rather clear and open language, which permitted the apprehension in time of all those involved in the plan and their conviction. It seems more likely that this was an emotional and noisy presentation than that it was an actual underground plan."

Bazak was quite clear on Kahane's personality, motives, actions, and methods: "... it is easier to deliver a verdict for an ordinary criminal, for whom the court has no sympathy... more difficult for a defendant whose aims are presumably lofty, but whose means are perverted and dangerous. It is all the more regrettable that the defendant proved in the speech delivered before the verdict that his position on what is permitted and forbidden in a democratic society has not changed... he does not acknowledge the fact that Israel's foreign and defense policy must be conducted by the government, which was elected by democratic process. According to him, he is permitted to conduct Israel's foreign and defense policy in his own manner, with no need of supervision or control. He presumably is incapable of ever erring... and therefore does not need the advice of experts, nor the prior approval of the society's authorized representatives. He determines policy, he is the implementor, he is the judge, and he is the critic.

"... an orderly society, especially a country such as the State of Israel, engaged in a bitter struggle with its enemies, cannot permit a private individual, no matter how good his intentions, to conduct its foreign and defense policy in its stead, even by nonviolent means, and surely not by means [involving] destruction and death.

"If the defendant does not become aware of this himself, I do not think that he will change his ways as a result of several months imprisonment. The only remaining way would be to imprison him for an extended period, thus denying him the possibility of continuing on his dangerous path.

"In determining the defendant's punishment this time, it should be remembered that he is primarily being punished for the act he committed, not for his anarchistic views... the act... was within the bounds of an attempt to commit a crime, since the letters were seized before they left the country. Had they left the country, it is not at all certain that the recipients would have accepted the proposals contained in them.

"Since the defendant has already been detained for a month in connection with the trial, it seems to me that the most fitting punishment would be a suspended sentence of imprisonment for an extended period, constituting a final and serious warning to the defendant to accept upon himself the laws of the State of Israel and the norms of its government, and not to exceed them."

Bazak gave Kahane a two-year suspended sentence; once again, a light rebuke.

16

The JDL and Kahane's Shuttle Diplomacy

Once Kahane immigrated to Israel, he could no longer exert continuous control over the American JDL, thereby losing his territorial base in New York. His followers, however, continued – as they still do – to harass foreign diplomats, particularly those from the Soviet bloc, Arabs, and PLO officials or sympathizers. But they played like a small, discordant orchestra that had lost its conductor and could credit no major achievements during the 1970's and '80's save a few sporadic violent outbursts that occasionally made headlines. While JDL spokesmen usually deny involvement in specific acts of violence, their denials are nearly always followed by endorsements of those acts.

During his first four years in Israel, Kahane was primarily involved with building up a following there: recruiting members, soliciting donations, touring, lecturing, airing his views, and organizing his first political campaign for election to the Knesset in 1973. He suffered bitter disappointments, particularly when he was defeated in those elections. The Israeli electorate did not want a racist in the Knesset in 1973.

From 1973 through 1975, Kahane was occupied by consultations with his lawyers, appearances in court, arrests, and time in jail. He was involved with an attempt to smuggle arms, the attempt to establish a miniature underground called "Terror against Terror" (referred to as "T.N.T.," the acronym formed from the Hebrew name of the organization), in response to the murder of the Israeli athletes at the Munich Olympics. While he found time to order his people in the United States to sabotage Soviet leader Leonid Brezhnev's visit, Kahane, himself, seldom visited the U.S.

After the burden of his trials in Jerusalem abated, Kahane once again was seen in New York. In January 1975, he and 47 followers were arrested after demonstrating in front of the Soviet mission to the United Nations. There was a violent clash at the demonstration; six people, including two policemen, were injured. On February 8, 1975, Kahane was charged with complicity in the attempted kidnapping of a Soviet diplomat and the bombing of the Iraqi embassy in Washington.

These charges, together with those he had incurred in Israel, clearly violated the terms of his suspended sentence in the U.S. A federal judge found him guilty and remanded Kahane to prison to serve the remaining year of his sentence. His prison term began on March 18, 1975. A month earlier, he had publicly announced that his organization (actually moribund at the time) planned to mobilize 150,000 volunteers for an army that would fight for Israel, emphasizing that the volunteers "would be prepared to kill Arabs if necessary."

In 1979 the JDL distributed a document inspired and authored by Kahane, that reveals much about the JDL and its leader: "Needed: An American Jewish Underground... (to) quietly and professionally eliminate those modern day Hitlers who are becoming an ever increasing threat to our very existence.... I state emphatically, the JDL is not an 'underground.' It is an 'above ground' organization, an activist, ideological movement which operates in full view of the public and police. Militant and sometimes violent? Yes, in the defense of Jews. But a void, a gap needs to be filled within the complex make-up of the American Jewish community today. As I stated above, what is needed is a secret underground strike-force which will eliminate those individuals that threaten our very existence. The time is long overdue for the birth of such a group."

In November 1979, under Kahane's directives, the JDL distributed the following announcement to the press: "The Jewish

100

Defense League urges American Jews to purchase firearms and know how to use them as part of the forty-first observance of Kristallnacht, or 'Night of Broken Glass,' in which pogromlike rioting was directed against the Jewish communities of Germany on November 9th and 10th, 1938.

"Stating that 'America closely resembles the Germany of the 1920's,' and that 'overt and physical Jew-hatred covers nearly the entire spectrum of American society today,' JDL National Director Bert Becker announced the JDL would begin the 'Every Jew a .22' campaign on the anniversary of Kristallnacht."

While he was in prison, Kahane announced that he was forming a Jewish "counter-terrorist group" in order to "combat the sworn enemies of the Jewish people with hard-core violence." He promised that the JDL would serve his new organization "as a conduit in relaying their views and plans to whoever they would ask us to; to serve as an ideological and philosophical guide for them, and to aid them in whatever way we can." Like most of Kahane's "operations," this organization existed only on paper, and was primarily intended to attract publicity.

Kahane's voice began to fade. Prison put a damper on his activity. Silence reigned in Israel and in the JDL's centers in the United States.

Kahane's voice was heard once again on April 13, 1976. He praised those followers who continued to attack Soviet diplomats as "Jewish patriots."

In November of 1976, five of Kahane's followers, inspired by their leader, conducted a five-hour sitdown in the offices of the Jewish Senator from Connecticut, Abraham Ribicoff. They were protesting Ribicoff's statements and stands on Israel. Kahane, who laid the groundwork for this action, had previously described the Senator, with customary hyperbole, as "a far greater danger to Israel than any Arab army."

Five days later, on November 24, Kahane led a small group in a sitdown at the offices of HIAS, to protest its decision to stop aiding Soviet Jewish emigrants who "dropped out" and decided not to go to Israel. They held posters and distributed fliers urging HIAS "not to cave in to Israeli pressure" on the issue.

By 1977, Kahane was back in Israel, once again running for the Knesset, and once again being soundly defeated, as Menahem Begin swept into power after 29 years in the opposition. While Kahane's activity in the United States was limited during the election year in Israel, he returned to the U.S. in time to stage yet another anti-Soviet demonstration. He was arrested, together with sixteen of his followers, for disturbing the peace by carrying signs and shouting anti-Soviet slogans at the Soviet national exhibit in the Los Angeles Convention Center. A JDL flier at the demonstration read: "Kahane has come from Jerusalem, Israel, to lead this demonstration. He fully expects to be arrested." Not surprising, since Kahane thrives on the publicity generated by his arrests.

By January of 1980, Kahane's Kach movement in Israel was responsible for violent incidents at Christian centers in Jerusalem. Members of the clergy were attacked. Arrests were made.

Kahane was arrested and placed under administrative detention the following May, after the police uncovered caches of arms and explosives stored by Kach in Hebron. A month later, the High Court of Justice rejected Kahane's request for release. The court did not disclose its full roster of charges against Kahane, commenting only that they were contingent on "a plot to attack Arabs."

On June 30, 1980, Kahane was sentenced to seven months' imprisonment, to run concurrently with his previous six-month sentence for disturbing the peace at the Hebrew University in 1979. On September 16, he was sentenced to an additional nine and one half months for disturbing the peace and for disorderly conduct in Ramallah and Nablus.

1981 was a relatively quiet year for Kahane who spent most of his time in prison.

Early in 1982, Kahane once more visited the U.S. On April 2, he and thirty of his followers took over the offices of the Herut movement in New York, protesting the Israeli withdrawal from Sinai. A week later, on April 9, they took over the offices of the Israeli Consulate in New York.

By June 1982, Kahane was back in Israel. A demonstration

was held protesting the Israeli invasion of Lebanon, Operation Peace for the Galilee. After urging his followers to beat up the demonstrators Kahane was arrested. He called the demonstrators "traitors," and told his people "go and get them."

On October 25, 1982, Kahane's followers illegally posted fliers extolling the massacre of Palestinians in the Sabra and Shatilla refugee camps, as "Divine retribution."

1983 was again a relatively quiet year; Kahane was occupied with preparations for the upcoming Knesset elections.

In 1984 Meir Kahane was elected to the Eleventh Knesset.

17

Kahane and the Electorate (1972–1985)

What led to Kahane's victory in 1984?

Upon emigrating to Israel in 1971, Kahane declared his aversion to participation in partisan politics. That declaration was abrogated the following year, when Kahane first decided to run for the Knesset. In December 1972, he asked the Kach secretariat for approval. The secretariat consisted of Kahane, Yossi Schneider, Barak Ben-Amos, Vladimir Ziberleib, and Yoel Lerner. Lerner and Ben-Amos opposed the Knesset race. Lerner explained that he had joined the movement only after assurances that it would center on ideology, not political campaigns; he reminded Kahane of his earlier promise to avoid partisan politics.

Kahane replied that he had changed his mind for two reasons: the desire for parliamentary immunity from police harassment and the need for funds (parties represented in the Knesset receive government funding in proportion to the number of MKs in the party). Finding a forum for his views proved no problem; newspapers, at the time, tended to be sympathetic.

Yet Kahane received only 12,811 votes in the 1973 elections, 0.81% of the total vote and less than the minimum necessary to enter the Knesset. Lerner, himself, voted for Menahem Begin. When Kahane was asked during his political campaign if a vote for him would not be wasted, he assured potential voters that a recent survey (conducted by Kahane, himself) had forecast his winning two Knesset seats. Indeed, he ran on the slogan, "Give us a third seat." The strategy proved counterproductive. Many potential voters, presumably convinced that Kahane could be elected without their vote, judged that one Knesset seat was sufficient for him, and cast their votes with Menahem Begin.

Nor was the campaign's fundraising effort successful. Kahane's American supporters resented his running for the Knesset. Contributions were low. Some 5000 names, purportedly on Kach's card index in Israel, were those of high school students, too young to vote. When Lerner broke with Kach in the summer of 1982, the card index contained only 85 names.

Kahane ran for the Knesset a second time in 1977. Results were even more dismal: 4,396 votes, a mere 0.25% of the total vote. Again, in 1981, Kahane received 5,128 votes, 0.26% of the total.

Yet in 1984, Meir Kahane received 25,907 votes, distributed among 545 localities in Israel. Following his victory in the Knesset elections, Kahane's strength rose in Kiryat Arba, a Jewish settlement overlooking Hebron. Indeed, the pattern of Kach's ascension to power in Kiryat Arba's local elections illuminates Kahane's impact on the national scene. During the settlement's local elections in 1980, not one member of Kach was elected to Kiryat Arba's municipal council. In Kiryat Arba's municipal elections of June 1985, however, Kach pulled 265 votes, 22.5% of the total. For the first time, two Kach representatives were elected to Kiryat Arba's eight-member municipal council. Kach was fourth in the city, following three other lists with strong nationalist platforms: Likud, Tehiya, and Morasha.

Why was Kach elected in 1984 and not in the preceding three elections?

Kiryat Arba is predominantly (80%) religious. School enrollment in 1984 registered 50–60 pupils in the nonreligious elementary school, with 700 pupils in corresponding grades of the state religious school and the even more Orthodox Talmud Torah.

Like other settlements in Judea and Samaria, the vote for Kach in Kiryat Arba was a protest vote. Supporters of the

Jewish underground presumably voted for Kahane; but others evidently also felt that the very existence of Arab antagonism towards Jews was being swept under the rug by the incumbent Likud government; they wanted a firmer policy adopted vis-a-vis Arab provocation in the territories.

"Arabs did not throw stones when the Alignment was in power," observes Shalom Wach, head of Kiryat Arba's Local Council. Alignment governments never permitted the formation of an infrastructure of instability, comments Wach. When the mood heated up, inciters were quickly expelled to Jordan and their demonstrations did not appear on television.

According to Wach and his colleagues in Kiryat Arba's leadership, support for Kach springs from the government's failure to provide security, an extremely sensitive issue for the settlers. They agree that the IDF may have had its own problems in Lebanon, but do not see it as an excuse for the government's powerlessness. A stronger hand in the territories would squelch rock throwing, they argue, insisting that families who harbor rock throwers must be expelled.

Residents of Kiryat Arba, like those throughout Judea and Samaria, suggests Wach, have difficulty distinguishing between Kach and the Tehiya party. Tehiya focuses on one issue: settlement throughout Eretz Israel (the Land of Israel). While Kahane also champions this cause, he finds the issue more complex. At the same time, his formulations for dealing with it are simpler and hence, more extreme. Kahane relates to Zionism's central message, explains Wach, but he devotes himself entirely to those obstacles which interfere with it: the Arabs and demography. That is the source of his weakness, Wach adds.

"Each of us has a Kahane in his head, an opening," suggests Wach. "Kahane can thus infiltrate the heads of many in Israel, including those on the left. The difference between Kahane and the left is simple: Kahane thinks that Israel has another opportunity to expel the Arabs, while the left despairs of such an opportunity."

Will Kahane become a permanent feature on the Israeli landscape?

For Wach and his colleagues, the answer depends primarily

on how the government conducts itself. If it shows minimal self-respect, in their terms, by offering support for Jews and punishment for those "who throw rocks at children in school-buses, the phenomenon of Kahane would vanish. If Israel guards the border with Jordan," they argue, "it must also guard the Jews in Eretz Israel."

The people of Kiryat Arba speak of a "second factor" that brought Kahane into the Knesset: the need for a voice raised in opposition to the left. They argue that the triumvirate of Yossi Sarid, Shulamit Aloni, and the Progressive List for Peace, whom they dub "the screamers", are "sinking democracy. Someone like Kahane has to be positioned against them, a scarecrow, a trumpet who will shout at them ceaselessly. So that there will be some sort of balance."

Yet Shalom Wach is exceedingly disturbed by Kahane. He insists that Kahane was not elected for ideological reasons, but rather in reaction to a "vacuum" on Israel's political map. Kahane's rise does not indicate a growing philosophy of racism on the part of the electorate, Wach maintains; it is merely a protest against extremists of the left.

Today, even Tehiya vacillates, according to Wach. MK Geula Cohen's apearance in Kiryat Arba on the eve of 1984 elections "only gave more votes to the unequivocal, decisive Kahane, when Cohen condemned the Jewish underground."

"The powerlessness of the Likud government in all areas is responsible for Kahane's election to the Knesset," Wach reiterates. "Yosef Burg was revealed to be good for nothing as Minister of the Interior and Police. Attorney-General Yitzhak Zamir was not forceful in his recommendations. This created a chain reaction: the underground, and after that, Kahane in the Knesset. At times I feel weak when I hear Kahane. I don't know who's normal here..."

For most settlers in Kiryat Arba the Kach victory springs from the government's "failures" in its war against terror and in its protection of the roads in Judea and Samaria from attacks and stone throwing by Arabs. The release of 600 Palestinians, most of whom are terrorists and murderers, as part of the agreement for the release of the three Israeli POW's held by Ahmed Jibril's organization, also increased Kahane's strength in Judea and Samaria. Most of the murderers returned to their homes, and pose a potential threat to the Jewish settlers, who seek refuge with Kahane. The Jews in Kiryat Arba, close to Hebron (known for its massacre of Jews in the past), want an extremist approach to Arab disturbers of the peace and terrorists. There are many former Americans and newly-religious Jews in Kiryat Arba who were followers of Kahane when they were still in the United States. Others were disappointed with the Likud government, and its failure to fulfill the settlers' expectations.

Shalom Wach and Eliakim Ha'etzni, who is nonreligious, did not mind signing a coalition agreement with Kach, which stated that Arab workers would not be employed in the municipal council and its institutions, that there would be public observance of the Sabbath, and that the swimming pool would be sex segregated.

The Kach list in Kiryat Arba was run behind the scenes by Baruch Marzel, Kahane's parliamentary secretary and one of his most extreme followers. Marzel has been arrested several times for attacks on Arabs. He lives in Tel Rumeida, in Hebron. The Kach list in Kiryat Arba is headed by Rami Zayit, a former kibbutznik from Hanita on the Lebanese border. Zayit is newly-observant, and a political innocent. "Kach didn't have a representative," remarked Zayit, "so they took a free ride on me. I'm not anti-Kach, but I voted for Tehiya in the last Knesset elections."

Kahane's present and past associates predict a further rise in Kahane's electoral strength. Yossi Schneider suggests that Kahane will win three to four seats in the Knesset before he can be stopped. Avner Uzan talks of Kach receiving six seats in the Knesset and forming a coalition with the Likud. Gad Servetman, the current Kach spokesman, sees Kahane as Defense Minister in 20 years.

A public-opinion poll was conducted by the Modi'in Ezrahi research institute one year after Kahane's election to the Knesset. Those polled, a cross-section of Israeli Jews (excluding kibbutzim and the residents of Judea, Samaria, and the Golan Heights), were asked for whom they would vote if elections were held now. The response was amazing. The Alignment received 51 seats (up from the 40 it received in the 1984 election), the Likud dropped to 24 seats (down from 31 in the current Knesset), and Kahane jumped to third place, with Kach receiving 11 seats in the Knesset.

In order to regain its standing as sole flagbearer of the right, the Likud would have to be headed by a popular, charismatic figure to cancel Kahane's inroads. Ariel Sharon, Defense Minister during the Lebanon war, and currently Industry and Trade Minister in the National Unity Government, demands the leadership of the Likud for himself, arguing that only he can return the Likud to power and eject Kach from the Knesset. Sharon warned his followers at the Bat Yam branch of Herut in July 1985: "Our danger is not Yossi Sarid, but rather Kahane, who takes all our votes."

On December 18, 1984, five months after Meir Kahane was elected to the Knesset, the Knesset Committee voted to restrict Kahane's parliamentary immunity. The motion was supported by twelve MKs from the center and the left – the Alignment, Mapam, the CRM, Shinui, and Rakah (the Democratic Front for Peace and Equality). The 8 MK's from the right and the religious party – Likud, NRP, Tehiya – voted against the motion. On December 25, 1984 the Knesset voted as a whole on the motion to restrict Kahane's parliamentary privileges for freedom of movement. In a secret vote, the Knesset voted to restrict Kahane, by a vote of 58 to 36.

Kahane's reaction to the Knesset vote came as no surprise. He referred to the bill's two sponsors, Yossi Sarid and Edna Solodar, as "SS." He later informed the Knesset that it had "fallen prisoner to the leftist terror," and ended with his usual pathos: "Whoever is for the L-rd, to me [the rallying cry of the Hasmoneans in their revolt against the Hellenizers from Syria – trans.]. Now vote. I'm going to recite the *Minhah* prayer."

The deliberation preceding the vote in the Knesset was quite revealing. The strong condemnations of Kahane by MK's from the right end of the Israeli political spectrum are of particular significance. Geula Cohen, of the rightwing Tehiya party, stated, "every one of us wants as little Kahane as possible....

There is another racist party in the Knesset besides Kahane, called the Progressive or retarded List for Peace. It is also a party which serves here as a real official representative of the PLO.... What bothers me is not only MK Kahane's freedom of movement in Arab villages, but also his freedom of movement in Jewish settlements, and his freedom of speech in the Knesset also bothers me. We therefore have to deal with this matter in a much more practical way. I don't know if there is anybody who wants ... as little Kahane as possible more than I do, since he explicitly reveals racism; when a person says in the Knesset, 'Shut up, Arab,' there aren't too many ways to interpret this. Of course, we have to add his incitement encouraging Jewish terror. I have an additional reason which bothers me in this context, and that is the great damage which he causes to [Jewish] settlement in Judea and Samaria.... Do you think that all those who stream after Kahane know all the laws on racism which have been read out here? Those who stream after him do so since it seems to them that he provides an answer to the subject of Arab terror, and that he redeems our national honor.... I say to them that Kahane is against the Jews, and that he will cause repression here for the Jews, within this land. I'm speaking about his racist side. They don't know this. There is a great deal of confusion among them.... I am sure that even those who voted for him to this Knesset don't know who this man is.... Kahane will deal mainly with the Jews. He wants to establish a repressive regime here which will cancel all freedoms, in accord with his distorted understanding of Jewish law.... My claim against Kahane is that he wants to turn the State of Israel into another dictatorial Khomeinistic Arab state, like those around us, and I'll fight against this."

Ronni Milo, one of the sharper tongues in Likud, was no less harsh in his evaluation of Kahane: "...In my eyes, Kahane is a racist, whose style and expressions are abominable.... In my opinion, the problem of Kahane is not a political problem, but, a public, educational problem.... Perhaps we should amend the proposal and decide that before we pass judgement we should send him for psychiatric observation. Let us receive a psychiatric opinion before we judge the man, since he's crazy...."

110

After warning of the threat to Israeli democracy posed by Kahanism, Jacques Ya'akov Amir (Alignment) offered an explanation for the rise of Kahanism: "Every time that Jews are murdered, this arouses all kinds of latent emotions within us; who does not have such emotions from his childhood, when he walked around and saw all kinds of camps...."

Benyamin Ben-Eliezer (Yahad) added a professional opinion of the results of Kahane's actions: "I won't be wrong if I say that, in my opinion, his manner of conduct and expressions harm, first of all, the security of the State of Israel. I have much experience with him as [military] commander of Judea and Samaria, as well as Coordinator of Activities in the Territories; I won't be wrong if I say that he causes harm of the first degree even to the [Jewish] settlers themselves." Ben-Eliezer added that the IDF had limited Kahane's freedom of movement in the past (in September 1972 IDF commanders forbade Kahane to enter Judea, Samaria, and the Gaza Strip – Y.K.), "since we saw that his continued freedom of movement was a danger to security." Pointing to Kahane's incitement of residents of development towns, Ben-Eliezer read from a letter by Shlomo Bukhbut, the head of the Ma'alot Tarshiha Regional Council (a mixed Jewish-Arab city in the Upper Galilee): "...the residents of the two settlements are generally quiet and peaceful residents, loyal to the State. MK Kahane appeared a few days ago, and incited against the Arabs in an insulting manner, in Ma'alot of all places, which symbolizes cooperation and fraternity between Jews and Arabs." He noted that Kahane's audience was composed mostly of youth, and stated that this was highly dangerous, "since it is specifically the youth, which is forming its self-image today, and the image of the State of Israel tomorrow, which will absorb the poison and venom which are stamped in the soul of this MK." Bukhbut closed his letter with a request for an urgent motion against racism.

Meir Kahane replied to the invitation to appear before the Knesset Committee in the following letter to the secretary of the committee: "Dear Madam, I received your letter of the 27th of [the month of] Tishrei in which you invite me to the lynching party which is supposed to discuss revoking my freedom of movement within the State.

"It is clear that I will not debase myself by appearing before the Committee. The leftist fascism has already made its mark in many ways, but it seems to me that it has excelled itself with this lynch. It is a pity that the Knesset has fallen into the hands of a Speaker who does not even attempt to hide his blind hatred of us.

"With the love of Israel, Rabbi M. Kahane, member of Knesset."

Attorney-General Yitzhak Zamir declared that Kahane's attempt to enter the Arab settlement of Taibe, "was intended as a provocation.... There is nothing preventing MK Kahane from entering an Arab village; no one told him he did not have permission to enter. What he did was to give prior notice to the entire public, to the police, and to the residents of the village, with the intent of creating ferment, disturbances, and disorder."

Zamir cited a judgement by former Supreme Court judge Tzvi Berenson, in which the judge noted that the Jewish people had suffered throughout its history in the Diaspora because of its different religion, and cautioned that they must therefore be exceedingly careful not to oppress minorities in their own state. Berenson stated that the hatred of foreigners destroys the image of God of the hater, and brings undeserved evil upon the foreigner. The judge's ruling concluded: "We must reveal a humane and tolerant attitude towards everyone created in the image of God, and maintain the great principle of the equality of all men in rights and obligations."

Zamir added that this was true not only of Israeli law, "but also of Zionism and Judaism." Zamir said that he and others had thought that Kahanism was a "sick, but marginal, phenomenon, and not dangerous," but this changed when Kahane was elected to the Knesset. Noting that tens of thousands of Israelis supported Kahane, Zamir declared, "Today this phenomenon contains a clear and immediate danger to the social order in Israel.... The time has come to act. The question is how to act." Zamir noted that Kahane, both before and after his election, was careful not to personally engage in violent activities; the danger posed by Kahane "was expressed in

112

the things he said, in the racist incitement which came forth from him, rather than by acts." Zamir concluded by stating that his response to the question put to him by members of Knesset about limiting Kahane's immunity was "absolutely positive," citing the authority granted the Knesset to take such action by section 13 of the law of immunity for members of Knesset, adding that Kahane was "misusing" his parliamentary privileges.

Kahane appealed the Knesset vote to limit his immunity. Referring to Kahane's claim that he had not been permitted to state his case before the Knesset Committee, the ruling judge stated: "It is intolerable that a member of Knesset would provide misleading information in his appeal." In April 1985, the High Court of Justice rejected Kahane's appeal to overrule the Knesset decision, and ordered Kahane to pay court costs in the amount of IS 500,000.

18

Racism in Nazareth

The new city of Upper Nazareth, initially established as a counterweight to the older Arab city of Nazareth below, exemplifies the recent surge of Kahane's popularity, together with the reasons underlying it: social, national, religious and ethnic agitation against the perceived threat of a growing Arab minority. In 1981, Kahane received only 3 votes in upper Nazareth; in 1984, his support increased to 301 votes.

Eighteen thousand Jews and 4,000 Arabs (some 600 families) live in Upper Nazareth. Another 50,000 Arabs live within a four-mile radius of the city. Old Nazareth is the largest Arab city within Israel's pre-1967 borders and the only one whose population has more than doubled since 1948. Today, close to 40,000 Arabs live in old Nazareth. The 18,000 Jewish residents of Upper Nazareth thus find themselves inthe midst of an Arab population of 100,000.

The purpose for founding Upper Nazareth in 1965 was twofold: to serve as a springboard for increasing the Jewish population of the Galilee, where the majority of Israel's Arab citizens live and to protect the Jezreel Valley from a recurrence of Arab attacks, such as those that were launched during Israel's War of Independence in 1948. However, it soon became clear that most of Israel's Jews were not attracted to the area.

Jews in Upper Nazareth have sold apartments to Arabs. By

the end of 1984, Arabs owned or rented more than 80% of the apartments in the city's first housing development, originally intended as housing for career army personnel. Local Jews dub the development "Arafat Estates."

Until 1975, two government agencies were active in stemming the influx of Arabs: the regional interministerial housing committee and the Housing Ministry. They ran checks on the social and security backgrounds of anyone who wanted to move into the city. When apartments were vacated by Jews leaving the city, the Housing Ministry purchased the apartments, renovated them, and resold them to Jews. At that time, 534 Arab families lived in Upper Nazareth; the heads of households worked for the defense establishment, and their residence was considered a prize for their loyalty to the state.

For a variety of reasons, the housing committee was disbanded, easing the way for Arabs to move into the city. The Housing Ministry provided them with the forms of financial aid available for young couples and families living in overcrowded conditions. The first Arabs to arrive were related to those families connected with the defense establishment; they were followed by their relatives.

Many Jews in the city had financial problems and were not viably settled. Jobs were scarce; government assistance, scant. Friction simmered among the different Jewish ethnic groups living in the city. Many Jews simply gave up and began to leave. They preferred selling their apartments to Arabs, since Arab buyers were willing to pay 30–40% over market price.

In the summer of 1983, several Jews began to organize against what they termed "an Arab invasion." Alexander Finkelstein established MENA (an acronym formed from the Hebrew letters for "Defenders of Upper Nazareth). MENA's first impetus for action was generated by a petition from residents of one apartment building, calling for an end to the "Arab invasion." The residents were trying to prevent an Arab family from moving into one of the two vacant rental apartments in the 32-apartment building. The police were called in, and the Arab tenant obtained a restraining order. The Jewish residents were given 48 hours to come up with a legal means for blocking the

Arab's entry. A delegation, headed by Finkelstein, consulted then IDF's Chief of Staff Rafael Eitan, who lived in neighboring Tel Adashim. Eitan advised them to contact David Levy, Housing Minister and Deputy Prime Minister. Levy told the group that Arabs could live wherever they wanted.

In another instance, MENA received a call for help from an elderly woman, the only Jew remaining in a 16-apartment building inhabited by Arabs. She claimed that the Arabs were bothering her, and asked the group to assist her in finding a Jew to whom she could rent her apartment because she wanted to move to Tiberias. Finkelstein turned to the political parties, but they offered no help. The woman asked for $100 monthly rent, but MENA was successful in raising only half this sum in contributions.

As a last resort, Finkelstein turned to Kahane that summer. Two years earlier, Finkelstein and his wife had given Kahane two of the three votes he received in the city. Unlike the Alignment, Likud, and Tehiya, from whom Finkelstein had also requested aid. Kahane realized the electoral potential of such a move. It was agreed Kach and MENA would rent the apartment, opening up the Upper Nazareth branch of Kach in the apartment. In September 1984, a few months after the election, Kahane closed the Kach branch, claiming lack of funds. Nine of the other apartments in the building were owned by Arabs; six were rented by Arabs. MENA persuaded the owners of two apartments not to renew the leases of their Arab tenants, and eventually succeeded in housing a Jewish family in one of them.

There are only a few MENA and Kach activists in Upper Nazareth, perhaps a dozen in all. But they know how to make themselves heard, and the results show up in polling booths at election time.

The 301 votes that Kahane received in the 1984 elections were scattered throughout all 22 polling places in the city; Finkelstein had been active. He based his campaign propaganda on the claim that "the future of the State and our children is behind us. Our parents left us much after having made great sacrifices in foreign lands. They did not come to the Land of Israel specifically because of financial hardship or suffering."

116

Finkelstein fears that if present trends continue, the city will become Arab within 15 or 20 years. Most young people do not return to the city after completing their compulsory army service. Jobs vacated by Jews who are drafted are taken by Arabs, who are exempt from army service. Two thirds of the Jewish population is over 50, while the Arab population is composed mostly of young people. Arabs are attracted to Upper Nazareth's relatively high quality of life, given the overcrowding in lower Nazareth.

But Finkelstein calls this "a smoke screen for the Arab national goal of taking over the Jewish city." According to MENA, most Arabs who move to Upper Nazareth own land and property elsewhere. Examples cited include one former Arab policeman who bought nine apartments in the city and another Arab who presumably lives in Canada, but buys apartments to rent to Arabs in Upper Nazareth. Despite the government's allocation of land reserves for Arab Nazareth's expansion, says Finkelstein, "Arabs have set their eyes specifically on Upper Nazareth. The Housing Ministry built hundreds of apartments in a new development in Nazareth, Finkelstein points out, but they remained empty for three years, until – according to Finkelstein – Arabs learned that the rabbi of Mishmar Ha'emek planned to fill the development with religious Jews. At this point, exclaims Finkelstein: "The Arabs came immediately and settled in the development with the speed of a brushfire. Finkelstein "knows" that the Arabs want the land upon which Upper Nazareth was built returned to them. Those lands were expropriated from Arabs by British Mandatory authorities. He contends that their nationalist orientation is palpable, offering as evidence the fact that the "PLO-oriented" Progressive List for Peace received 200 votes in one Upper Nazareth polling place.

Kahane spent only IS 100,000 (about $300) for his 301 votes in Nazareth. Finkelstein's family and friends worked as volunteers. Kahane came to Upper Nazareth three times during the campaign. Finkelstein says hundreds came to hear Kahane, while the media reported audiences of "only dozens."

Alexander Finkelstein was born in Mandatory Palestine in

117

1928. His father had served in the Jewish military units in the British army in World War I. He himself served in the paramilitary Gadna youth movement and in the Palmah, the elite strike force of the pre-1948 Hagana. He served as security officer of Hula between 1955 and 1960, when he moved to Upper Nazareth. His wife immigrated from Rumania in 1955.

What does Finkelstein have against the Arabs?

According to Finkelstein, "Living next to Arabs harms the quality of life. Noise explodes all day and night from radios and televisions. Arab singing. Clans conduct visits. The lawn is dirty. Excessive use of the hall. It's a fact: since the establishment of the State, not one Jew has succeeded in living in the city of Nazareth proper, next to us. There are 42 Jewesses registered [i.e., living] in the Arab city [of Nazareth], mainly due to mixed marriages. Here as well, in Upper Nazareth, there are Jewesses from all communities who married Arabs, but there aren't any opposite cases: Jews don't take Arab wives for themselves. There aren't any hotels or restaurants in Upper Nazareth as there are in Arab Nazareth, down below. Tourists come mainly to the Arab city. Not a single dollar comes to Upper Nazareth from the visits of tourists in the lower city [Upper Nazareth is located on a hill overlooking Arab Nazareth], but they – the Arabs – come to live among us."

One MENA flier warns, "The entire country is Upper Nazareth. 'If you're not comfortable here, you can get up and go' – spoken by an Israeli citizen, a resident of Upper Nazareth, your neighbor Rita Huri. Do you have any place to which you can go?? Will the eternal "Wandering Jew" continue to wander, even in his own land?? Who said that the Arabs were the first in Nazareth?? Will you want your children tomorrow to learn the Koran or the New Testament?? Will you want to suddenly discover that your grandchildren are no longer Jewish?? Is wanting to continue being a free, Zionist, Jew racism?? Will you sell your identity to whoever offers the highest price?? Do you know the source of the money with which your property is purchased?? Will burying your head in the sand solve the problem?? What was the end result of the "good neighbor" [relationship] in Hebron in 1929 [when the Jewish community

118

was massacred]?? What will all the 'bleeding hearts' say when the problem reaches their doorstep?? Do the journalists from Ramat Hasharon, Herzliya [rich suburbs of Tel Aviv], and Tel Aviv represent your opinions? Will they save us from a national Holocaust?? All the slanders in the press and over the ether are intended to blur the real answers to the questions which we have asked you. Our minds are firmly made up, our stand is strong, and our way is clear, despite all the blind and the deaf defeatists, who try to distort the face of Zionism! Remember: tomorrow, the entire country will be Upper Nazareth – where will you go???"

Another poster announced a "Jewish Land Day" (as opposed to Arab Land Day), in order to protest against the following: the sale and rental of apartments in Upper Nazareth to Arabs; "the danger to the existence of Upper Nazareth as a regional capital in the heart of a **non-Jewish** Galilee: the danger of the loss of Jewish identity with the increase of mixed marriages; the social, religious, and cultural implications for our future and the future of our children as a result of the massive takeover of the city by Arabs"...

Yet another flier, sent at the beginning of 1985 to communities throughout Galilee and the northern part of the country, and to members of Knesset and other public figures, clearly reveals the blend of MENA's original purpose preventing Arabs from settling in Upper Nazareth with Kahane's themes of Arab sexual crimes and intermarriage: ...our property, homes, streets, and lands, which are drenched with the blood of our sons, are being sold, leased, and rented to Arabs! Our daughters, may God protect them, are raped and abandon themselves to prostitution! Intermarriages have lately increased in an alarming manner! Who is behind this serious development?... **Jews**: do you know that Afula has been conquered by the Arabs – jobs and industry, as well as a partial [takeover] of the moshavim and kibbutzim.

Still, Alexander Finkelstein isn't an exact copy of his teacher and master, Meir Kahane. In an interview with me, he's critical of Kahane's attacks on the left, the kibbutzim, and the Palmah. He wants Kahane to concentrate on the present and the future, and not on settling historical accounts. Finkelstein mentions that many families from the left have lost sons in Israel's wars, and says Kahane shouldn't make generalizations. He says that the left (i.e., the kibbutzim) "opposes the sale of Jewish property to Arabs, and hopes to gain their sympathy. Why does Kahane burn bridges to the left? Finkelstein asks. "Yossi Sarid is more honest than his former colleagues in the Alignment, each of whom has tens of faces. Sarid at least is consistent."

I remind him that, like Kahane, he himself preaches expulsion of Arabs by force, if necessary.

"No one is talking about the expulsion of the Arabs, but rather about a comprehensive agreement, anchored in law and international law, according to precedents. We absorbed the Jews from Arab countries who were dispossessed of their property. Let the Arabs of Israel move to the Arab lands, where they will assist in strengthening the economy. Then they will serve as the nucleus for cooperation."

– Why should they be sent away from here at all? Aren't they Israeli citizens like Jews?

"For us, Israel is a matter of existence. To be or not to be. We have to amputate the infected limb. Many ways have to be used for a population transfer, a deliberation [has to be conducted] on the property left here by the Arabs who fled during the time of the war [of Independence] and by the Jews who left and came here. I'm not pleased by Kahane's desire to put the Arabs to hard work. We have to be sophisticated and careful to solve the problem. In order to win support, there will have to be intensive information and groundwork. The Arab minority is growing stronger, and sticks in our throat."

Finkelstein strongly justifies the demonstration which Kahane organized in Um el-Fahum in August 1984. He describes the Arab village as "nationalistic, and demonstrated hatred towards the Jews in the 1936 riots." He recalls that Yusif Abu Dora, the head of the Arab gangs in the village, was hanged by the British. "The Arabs have tremendous stores of arms. Whenever a quar-

rel breaks out among them, they quickly take out IDF arms."
He says large quantities of arms were found in the village. He
favors frontal actions such as the demonstration in Um el-
Fahum, claiming they aid in pinpointing inciting elements
among the Arabs. "It's enough to grab several inciters in each of
their demonstrations, so that they'll sing and surrender their fellow activists, and reveal their plans, point out the sources of
their weapons."

Finkelstein listens to the Arabs. He finds that the "average
Arab" fears Kahane because of the possibility of his transfer
program becoming a reality, but "deep down, respects him."
Finkelstein has a simple explanation for this: "The Arabs know
that they deserve what Kahane says and wants to do, since the
Jews are the owners of the country." It follows from this that
Kahane terrifies them, and that they have begun to moderate
their statements, if not their opinions.

Several Arab families from the Galilee village of Iksalt came
to Finkelstein, Kahane's representative in Galilee. He says that
they told him, "Israel belongs to you. There will be bloodshed
here. We want to finish off quietly." Finkelstein was quick to
send their request to Kahane's secretary in Jerusalem, but there
was no response. Finkelstein himself is not as generous as
Kahane. He's willing to give the Arabs who leave the country
compensation, but only as part of a package deal, in return for a
similar arrangement for Jews from Arab lands, who were
"expelled and whose property was expropriated."

Kahane's popularity appears to be rising, especially among
the young, including high school students. A poll conducted in
1985 by Dr. Kalman Benyamini, of the Hebrew University,
revealed that 50% of the respondents (high school students in
the eighth through twelfth grades) favor cancelling Arabs rights;
the trend towards the simplistic solutions proposed by Kahane is
increasing. Finkelstein explains that Kahane's conception "is
latent among many Jews in all the parties. All of them fear for
the future of the country, but the magic formula, which will put

his teachings into practice, has not yet been discovered, and I lose sleep over this. The more his popularity grows, the more successful he'll be, and the Arabs will give us a reason to support Kahane more and more."

Yet Finkelstein is uneasy about Kahane's religiosity; he opposes religious coercion, but favors coercive measures against Arabs.

"Kahane's movement today is flimsy. A solid leading team has to arise." Finkelstein may be unaware of Kahane's history: both in the United States and in Israel, Kahane's movements, have always been based on his personal whims alone.

The Upper Nazareth activist is optimistic about the future: "Even MK Yossi Sarid will join Kach in twenty years. He won't have any other choice." He predicts Kahane will double or triple his hold on the city in future elections.

19

Israeli Disciples

Avner Uzan

Kahane's activists are scattered throughout Israel, in the territories as well as within pre-1967 borders. They contend with Gush Emunim and the Tehiya party for the mind of the Israeli who lives in Judea, Samaria, or Gaza. The Likud is in retreat; the trend moves towards extremism.

I met Avner Uzan at the end of September 1984 in Ariel, a new city in Samaria. Uzan, one of Kahane's most devoted followers, was fourth on the Kach list in 1984, and serves as Kahane's bodyguard. He sat beside Kahane at the press conference in which his leader presented a Jewess who had been given shelter by Uzan after leaving her Arab husband. Uzan, like others in Kach, is an underground unto himself, conducting secret operations against Arabs either by himself or with the aid of others in the movement. Kahane does not always know of these operations, but he always gives them his ex post facto approval and blessings.

Uzan was born in Hadera in 1958, and grew up in an agricultural settlement near Natanya. Like the rest of his family, he was active in Betar as a youth. As a teenager, he acted as a counselor for street gangs, on a volunteer basis. He served as a military policeman during his compulsory military service, a role for which his muscular physique was well-suited. For a year he helped his father, growing flowers, oranges, and pecans. The farm flourished. Uzan also found a well-paying job as a tenured driver for the Dan bus cooperative. His territory included the lines throughout Samaria. In 1980 he maried Zahava, born in Beersheva. The two had met during army service in El Arish, in the Sinai peninsula. They lived for three years in a tiny prefab apartment in Ariel before moving to a new settlement in the territories.

Avner had been enthusiastic about Kach since his youth. He was afraid that he would have difficulties in being accepted into its ranks; he thought of it as a secret movement. He joined Kach in 1978 when he completed his compulsory service in the IDF, although he had voted for the Likud in the 1977 elections. He had not wanted to break the family tradition of voting for Menahem Begin. He began his activity in Kach by distributing fliers. It was only in 1982 that he became a central figure in the party, culminating in his inclusion on the party's Knesset list for the 1984 elections. When we spoke, Uzan was serving as metropolitan Tel Aviv coordinator for Kach, operating out of a Tel Aviv office. He directed 200 activists during the campaign. After the elections he was forced to leave his post as coordinator to lecture before small groups in private homes, mainly in Samaria, but also within Israel proper.

Kahane received 17 votes in Ariel in the 1984 elections, and the Alignment received a surprising 50 votes; most of Ariel voted for the Likud. Uzan and his fellow activists in Kach felt good after Kahane's election. His job as a bus driver gives him an opportunity to listen to passengers. He's happy about the public's response. People are no longer ashamed to talk about Kach, he says everyone knows who Kahane is. Whether for good or bad, they talk about him; they relate to him. They know what he wants. The activists have achieved part of the goal they set for themselves. Uzan expects Kahane to receive five or six seats in the next Knesset elections. If it were dependent on him or on Kahane, they would call new elections "immediately."

Uzan describes Kach as a "national-religious" movement,

most of whose voters and activists are nonreligious. He claims that Kach's voters are "a cross section of the people," and include university professors, pilots in the Air Force, former kibbutz members, youth, and many soldiers. All of these groups are nonreligious. Uzan explains this seeming contradiction by citing the passage "And let them make Me a sanctuary that I may dwell among them" (Ex. 25:8), explaining that the fact that "among them" is in the plural, while the word "sanctuary" is in the singular, teaches that "a sanctuary dwells among each one of the Jewish people, and there is a warm spot for Judaism within him."

Like many in Kach, he grew up in a nonreligious home, but later became an observant Jew. He sports a thick black beard and a small skullcap. Most of the passengers on his route, the Tel Aviv-Alon Moreh (in Samaria) run, are religious. At first he regarded them as "dummies," but they slowly began to interest him. He learned about their way of life and thought. "Today I live like them, and live better than in the past." His parents were influenced by him and began to observe the Jewish dietary laws. He himself studied with the rabbi of Alon Moreh.

Uzan once had great hopes for the Likud, but its leaders disappointed him. He and his friends concluded that when the Alignment was in power, it curbed the Arabs more firmly. The Likud did not prevent stoning of Israeli vehicles. His bus goes through Nablus six times a day. Stones were thrown at his bus; he responded by firing shots in the air. The Likud remained apathetic. The demonstration of its weakness in dealing with Arab disturbers of the peace in the territories pushed many voters towards Kach. Uzan maintains the process will continue. The coverage that Kach and Kahane receive in the media "granted us legitimacy. Now we'll have more members of Knesset."

His thoughts on the changing reality in Israel may be a pipe dream no longer. "The philosophy of expelling Arabs can be put into practice. When we have six seats in the Knesset, and we form a coalition with the Likud, the Likud will have commitments towards us. We will demand the establishment of a government body authorized to deal with the emigration of

Arabs, Israeli Arabs. The official in charge of this department will travel to, say, Canada. He will deal with the absorption and settlement of the Arabs there. Everything will be done with compensation. We will purchase the land and house of the migrating Arab. American Jews will also contribute. Sixty-five percent of the population of Jordan are Palestinians. The rest are Beduin. Jordan is Palestine. It will be possible to transfer the Arabs there, or to disperse them throughout the world."

– And if they won't want to leave of their own free will?

"We'll bring them to this. If we don't take them out of here, they'll take us out."

The campaign against the Arabs will begin in another five years. The reason? "First they'll finish building Judea and Samaria for us." Then the builders will be expelled, "since we're degenerating due to them." He wants the Jews to return to physical labor. "The Arabs don't appear for work – cleaning buses – on their holidays. I volunteered to clean 30 buses by myself."

No, he doesn't hate Arabs. He's only being "realistic." "I'm not filled with hatred for Arabs, but rather concern for our future. They multiply four to one. If they continue to increase like this, we'll have 40 Tawfiq Toubis [a member of Knesset from the Democratic Front for Peace and Equality list] in the Knesset. I'm worried by the Arab student who studies with me in Tel Aviv University. The Arabs won't agree to live under a Jewish minority which will rule them if they increase rapidly. We have to stop before the chasm."

When he was in the home of his farmer parents he "paid attention" to the behavior of the Arab workers in the settlement, who were needed to pick the citrus crop. The Jews didn't show up, they preferred collecting unemployment pay to working. This was after the Six-Day War. He was a boy at the time. The Arabs came from Taibe. He saw them at work, talking, eating, drinking, and saw how they "divided among them our property. When you show a bit of weakness towards them, they'll be quick to stick a knife in your back, turn it, and afterwards lift up the injured person in order to tear him to pieces."

He's full of experiences from his duty in the reserves. He served in a prison for terrorists near Nablus. The prisoners used to make fun of him. They cursed and spat. Uzan shuddered. His Jewish-national pride was seriously hurt. He couldn't bear the humiliation and the shame. He tried to get to know the leaders of the prisoners. They received personal care from him. "After they were properly 'softened up,' they were quiet. They stopped complaining, even about the presumed shortage of food, to the representatives of the International Red Cross. Everything was in perfect order. They were satisfied. The Arab only understands force, but today they ride on us in the territories, and we turn the other cheek."

– Are you in favor of a state run in accordance with Jewish religious law?

"Yes."

– By force?

"No. If rabbis teach the Bible in secular schools, the population will slowly absorb religious values, and we'll get to a religiously-run state in a democratic fashion."

– What do you think about Kahane?

"He is a figure to identify with, but there are those who prefer Motta Gur [Alignment Minister of Health] or Yossi Sarid [Citizens' Rights Movement member of Knesset, known for his dovish views]. When I joined the movement I didn't know Kahane. Nor did I know those who came from deprived homes. We have good youth in Kach, many of them from Bnei Akiva [the religious Zionist youth movement], but money is needed to organize the youth. I proposed tours at half-price, but even for this there isn't money. The movement doesn't even have money to repay what I spent on it (during the 1984 elections) – IS100,000 [a few hundred dollars]. There are idealists in the movement."

– How do they mobilize you for action?

"Like a mobilization notice for reserve duty. They phone and tell you about an activity, a demonstration. I go to Petah Tikvah to my supporters there and bring forty people. Uriel Vahab, from Rosh Ha'ayin, mobilizes activists in a flash. He owns a carpentry shop. He stops his work and comes as a volunteer.

127

Five full buses came to Um el-Fahum. The meeting point was near Hadera. We went from there in an organized manner. Why did we go there? We wanted to go for an outing in the country."

He is contemptuous of the media. "It only strengthens us." He draws an analogy with what "they are doing to [Ariel] Sharon. They defame him. They call him a murderer, a criminal, a thief, but he received 42% of the votes at the Herut convention. The press doesn't reflect the truth. The people made itself immune to it a long time ago. It determines what is good and what is bad. The journalists won't determine [this] for me. The ideas come from the rabbi [Kahane]. He's a great, open, man. A wise man. He thinks in every direction. He accepts criticism, viewing it as constructive, not destructive. Once I shouted at him about his careless outward appearance before the filming of election commercials. He took account of this and improved his dress."

– Do you have secret, underground, activities?

"On Thursday, September 6, 1984 [the interview was conducted at the end of September – Y.K.], I went with —— from Kach to Um el-Fahum to distribute fliers at night. We were supposed to go into the city. I coordinated the action with my partner by telephone. We wanted to write slogans on the walls of the houses. We arrived. We saw a police roadblock positioned at the city's entrance. We immediately continued on to Upper Nazareth to visit a friend. It was 1:30 a.m. When we left Upper Nazareth we saw that the police roadblock was still in place. We didn't give up. We parked the Fiat in the nearby settlement of Mei Ami. It was three o'clock in the morning. We went on foot. We crossed the hill. We reached Um el-Fahum. We distributed the fliers and fled. We saw the Border Police there. We left fliers near the post office, Bank Hapoalim, the bus station. They were written in Hebrew. When I went out to the action from my house there were police spread from Rosh Ha'ayin to Um el-Fahum.

"I returned home from Mei Ami at about 4 in the morning. First I brought my friend back to his house. We cleaned the car of anything incriminating. I drove onto the cross-Samaria highway. There was a police roadblock there. They politely waved me on. They thought that I intended to act in Kfar Kassem. They apparently saw the fliers which we had left in Um el-Fahum. I passed Kfar Kassem on my way home to Ariel. I was stopped by a police roadblock at the exit from the village [Kfar Kassem]. I saw in my rear-view mirror that a patrol car without lights was following me. They told me, 'Pull over. Shut off your lights. Open the engine compartment. Open the trunk.' I stated on my radio that they had arrested me. After a wait of ten minutes, the deputy commander of the Petah Tikvah police [station] arrived, along with detectives and uniformed policemen. It was 4:30 a.m. They conducted searches. They found my licensed pistol in the car. They didn't find fliers. I recently completed army reserve duty. I still had two M-16 magazines. I was arrested for possession of IDF equipment. It was an excuse. The deputy commander conducted the search himself. He's a superintendent. They put three detectives in my car. The police escort travelled after me. We arrived at the Petah Tikvah police station. They took testimony from me. They confiscated the magazines. They also confiscated posters which we had prepared for the demonstration for the soldier Moshe Tamam who had been murdered [Tamam, who lived near Natanya, was kidnapped and murdered when he hitchhiked home on leave from the army at the beginning of August 1984. He was unarmed. His body was found in Samaria – Y.K.], such as 'Jewish Blood Is Not Cheap.' There were also posters for Rabbi Kahane's lectures. They placed me in detention. I was there from 4:30 a.m. until 3:00 p.m. the next day, Friday. They imprisoned me in a cell together with criminals. I was released on IS 5,000 bail, which was raised by Uriel Vahab of Rosh Ha'ayin.

"The investigators asked me, 'What are you doing at such a late hour on the road?'

I said, 'Going for a ride.'

"We explained in the fliers why we want the Arabs to emigrate. Each flier had a coupon in which the reader was asked to fill in the details necessary for emigration. Responses arrived. In order to walk around in an Arab village at night, we took off our skullcaps and gave up wearing our ritual fringes. We were dressed sloppily, like Arabs."

– Was the action done with Kahane's approval?

Uzan smiles instead of answering. Then he says, "A spontaneous action," and smiles once again.

The day after the action, Uzan learned from a senior police officer that police had been stationed throughout the entire area after the telephone conversation he had with his partner on the secret action.

– What are your underground activities against Arabs?

"We saved about 100 Jewesses who had turned to prostitution because of drugs. There are members among us in Kach who go out on violent actions to save Jewish girls who fall prey to Arabs, who hook them on drugs. Afterwards they become addicts, and they can be used for prostitution in Arab villages, as well as in other cities, such as Jaffa."

Uzan asks me to come down with him to his car parked in front of his house. He opens the trunk and shows me the special equipment he has for violent actions conducted by individuals and small squads within Kach. Behind the back seat, on the floor of the car, is a huge club, looking like a wooden hoe handle. "This is the equipment for rescuing Jewesses from Arabs." Those "rescued" are brought discreetly to a shelter for battered wives in Herzliyah.

When I ask him if Kahane is involved in the planning of violent actions, he laughs out loud. Nor does he answer when I ask if Kahane knew of the activities of the small underground group, composed of Kach members, which shot at an Arab bus on the road to Ramallah and damaged Arab property. The group, composed of newly-religious Americans, was caught, and its members are now serving time in the Tel Mond prison.

On August 26, 1984, about a month before I interviewed Uzan, he was involved in a violent incident with members of the Knesset, and hurt an MK from Shinui, Mordechai Virshubski. Virshubski and three other MK's (Yair Tzaban from Mapam, Mordechai Bar-On from the CRM, and Beni Shalita from the Likud) had come to Tel Mond prison to determine whether members of the Jewish underground were receiving treatment different from that accorded other prisoners. Uzan and others stood by the entrance to the prison to demonstrate against the

MKs who had come, according to Uzan at his trial, "to make worse the conditions of the the arrested members of the Jewish underground. Uzan threatened Virshubski (who is partially disabled) through his loudspeaker, in order to intimidate and anger Virshubski. Uzan said, among other things, "I'll take your other leg off, I'll pull out your tongue. We'll ready a grave for you, since one leg of yours already is in the grave."

I asked Uzan what he wanted from Virshubski then.

"I told him during the demonstration that just as they had cut off the legs of Bassam Shak'a, so would we cut off his tongue. I called him a PLO-ist and a supporter of terrorists. I was the one who kept people apart after things heated up. The brother of the murdered soldier, Moshe Tamam, began a fight with Virshubski's aides. I separated [them] and tore Tamam's brother's shirt. Twenty people came from Tamam's family. I was the only one from Kach. I distributed four Kach T-shirts to them. I organized the family and they came. There's a person who murders with a knife, and I have to chop off the hand which holds the knife, and there are demonstrators from Peace Now who came to Hebron to incite against the Jews. If Virshubski comes to Hebron on the Sabbath to demonstrate against the placing of the trailers which the settlers brought, he only incites Arabs. He causes the Arabs to think that Jewish blood is cheap. This is how Aaron Gross and the yeshivah students fell in Hebron. Therefore I have to cut off the tongue which incites the Arabs against the Jews. We settled accounts with him for the demonstration in Hebron. I also shouted 'PLO-ist' at Morele Bar-On, because his daughter is married to a PLO-ist. This is the education she received at home [an apparent reference to Bar-On's former role as IDF Chief Education Officer – E.L.]."

Uzan's trial began on November 30. Kahane was present at the trial, and emphasized that Kach financed Uzan's lawyer, Meir Shechter of Jerusalem. Uzan claimed that the MKs had called them "Nazis" and a "mob" after the demonstraters had shouted "Leftists out!" The defendant Uzan said: "I was insulted, since, all in all, we are interested in cleansing the country of Arabs, and are not murderers. We're willing to transport

131

Arabs into Jordan in air-conditioned buses."

The defense attorney argued that the defendant's language merely reflected the general quality of life in Israel: "The expressions 'PLO-ist,' 'Nazi,' 'maniac,' which members of Knesset use from the dais of the Knesset, have become an accepted norm in Israel, and members of Knesset intentionally use these expressions. The television and the media broadcast them; the bandying about of expressions of this sort is not an insult, but rather a response to views, and a member of Knesset has to be aware of this when he complains that he is being insulted."

The judge thought differently. On February 12, 1985, he sentenced Uzan to four months imprisonment, a suspended sentence of an additional four months, and a fine of IS50,000. The judge stated in his verdict that "only a step separates verbal from physical violence, and it undermines the foundations of enlightened society. There is nothing more serious, nor more harmful and insulting than these expressions, which were used about one who has been occupied in public service for close to twenty years, eight of them as a member of Knesset. Shouts such as 'I will take off your other leg' to a disabled person are insulting, humiliating, and offensive; they must be regretted and condemned. During the course of the trial, I did not find that the defendant showed remorse; he continued in the same fashion, and stubbornly referred to MK Yair Tzaban by an unfitting expression ["the fat one"]. It is no wonder that MK Virshubski was frightened by those threats, when the defendant called out, 'We will take off your leg like we took off the legs of the Arab mayor."

Uzan appealed his sentence. The appeal was rejected.

"Eli"

"Eli" (at his request, his name has been changed) is the head of the Kach branch in one of Israel's largest Sephardic communities. He's been self-employed since 1978, and makes a good living. He was born in 1955 in Israel. His parents came fom an Arab country. He has three brothers and three sisters. He is married with four children. Until 1984 he voted for the Likud. In 1984 he voted for Kach, and was very active in the campaign. Kach received 300 votes in the town, while Tami, an ethnic list, dropped sharply to 200 votes. A huge poster hangs in his workshop, with Meir Kahane in its center. Kach publications, mostly press clippings of Arab assaults on Jewesses, lie next to the poster.

– Why did you vote for Kach?

"Because of the Arabs. They're swindlers and scoundrels. They attacked my family. My sister fell victim to the Arabs."

His sister Leah (name changed) is religious. She studied at a vocational school that trains teachers. After completing her studies, she began teaching. She still lived at home with her mother; each day she went out to work and returned home at night. One day one of the counselors at Leah's school called and told Eli that his sister was conducting telephone conversations in Arabic. After a short investigation, Eli learned that his sister was dating Arabs. He began to be aware of her strange behavior. She returned late at night. She had left her job, but went "to work" every morning with her briefcase, so as not to arouse suspicion that she "really was going out with Arabs."

After following her Eli learned that she was meeting a 25-year-old Arab from Taibe at a hotel in a nearby city. This Arab "Abed" employed another Jewess as a prostitute. He was a pimp. Eli and his brothers went to the hotel to ambush Abed. He trapped the Arab and asked, "Are you looking for trouble? What are you doing with my sister?" The Arab suggested they go to his room to talk. He took out a knife, and asked Eli, "What do you want now?" "I want you to get away from my sister." The Arab answered, "If you're a man, try to take the knife away from me." Eli heard his brothers calling from the street. Two of them came up, and the frightened Arab promised that he would not see their sister any more.

Back at home, Eli called Leah and gave her a dressing down. She promised that she would not see Abed, who had ruined her life. They had had a passionate love affair. She had met him when she traveled on a bus to her work. After three months she fell in love with him. She thought that he was a nonreligious Jew, whom she would make observant, but he revealed that he was an Arab.

Despite her promises, Leah went back to meeting her Arab lover. Eli stopped believing her. He went out of his mind. He was the youngest brother in the family, and Leah was the youngest daughter. His brothers were indifferent. His mother relies only on Eli. Eli decided to lie in wait for his sister. Once she came home in a taxi. The Arab seemed to be sitting in the taxi, beside the driver. Eli called one of his friends for help. They chased the taxi in their car. They identified it near one of the kibbutzim in the area. Eli went to the driver, and his friend to the Arab. Eli explained that he had "business" with the Arab. The driver understood. Eli saw the driver looking at the license plate of the car that had been following his taxi. Eli told the Arab, "You have to get out of the taxi now, otherwise we'll tear you apart." The driver insisted that the Arab pay him the fare. Eli and his friend then put the Arab into their car. His friend sat in back with the Arab. They drove to their home town. They put him in the basement of Eli's workshop, and chained him, hand and foot. Eli consulted his brothers. It was 2:30 a.m. One of his brothers said, "Finish him off, get rid of him."

Eli was careful. "I weigh my actions." He remembered that the taxi driver had been looking at the license plate of his car. He knew the taxi belonged to a company in north Tel Aviv. He went back to the taxi stand in Tel Aviv, to ask the driver where he had picked up the Arab but really wanted to find out whether the driver would register a complaint against him. The driver wasn't at the stand. The owner of the taxi was there in his stead; he told Eli that he hated Arabs, and that Eli had nothing to fear. Eli returned to the basement. He decided that the Arab had to be soundly beaten, and this is what he did, together with the friend who assisted him in the kidnapping. They placed a gun to his forehead in order to intimidate him, and warned him not to dare come near Leah again. Then they searched him, and found a switchblade hidden on his leg, under his sock. He didn't respond when they asked him what he was doing with the knife. Afterwards Eli and his friend finished a bottle of cognac, so that they wouldn't know what they were doing. "We drank and hit, hit and drank." Finally, Eli cut the Arab's hands with a broken bottle. Now the Arab promised them that he would not come near the sister any more.

It was 8:30 a.m. "We had a Jewish heart, and we took the Arab to a restaurant in a nearby city." The three had a hearty breakfast. Once again Abed promised that he would not meet with the sister. They let him go. He did not register a complaint with the police. Eli knew he had already spent two years in prison for seducing girls for prostitution. "I thought that this was the end of the episode," but no. A week later, Abed called Eli's wife, and told her to prepare two coffins. He wanted to set a date for a meeting with Eli in the municipal cemetery. Eli's wife warned him that he would be the one to be buried in the coffin. Eli spoke with him on the telephone. Abed told him that if he had registered a complaint with the police, they would have put Eli in prison for fifteen years, but he preferred meeting with Eli at midnight in the cemetery. Eli and his friend, armed, waited at midnight in the municipal cemetery for the Arab, but he didn't show up.

A few months passed. The sister continued meeting Abed in secret. The surveillance of the pair continued. The Arab moved from one address to another, from city to city, so that he would not be discovered, but Eli was always on his trail. When Abed was sent to Ramle Prison for seducing Jewish girls for prostitution, Eli calmed down. One of the prison guards, who knew Eli, told him that his sister visited Abed in prison. Eli arrived at the prison together with his friend. "I was lucky. The guard at the entrance was a rightwinger and not a leftist, so he cooperated with me. I was disguised. I wore a wig and glasses. I wanted to grab my sister before the entrance to the prison. She recognized me from a distance despite my disguise and disappeared. The guard advised me to take her identification card and other documents, so that she would not be able to visit the jail, and that is what I did." Leah stopped visiting Ramle Prison for a year and a half. She worked as a housekeeper.

Abed was released from prison in April 1984. "I turned to the police for help, but we live in a democracy, and they told me that nothing could be done. I attached a listening device to the telephone in my house. I was amazed when I recorded that my sister was continuing to meet him. She sounded like she was in love with him, but he didn't sound like this. When our mother was in the house, Leah spoke to him in code, as if he were a female, my sister's girlfriend. They continued to meet in a nearby city, but I didn't know where. I knew a friend of the Arab and I asked him. This one would sell him drugs, mainly hashish. He was addicted to hashish. I got his telephone number. Then I located his home. He rented an apartment from Jews. We went to the apartment, but he had managed to flee. My sister wasn't there.

"After the Arab was released from prison, I tried to rehabilitate my sister. I took her to a seminar with Uri Zohar [an Israeli actor who recently became extremely religious, abandoning his career as an entertainer] in a city in the southern part of the country. The newly-religious gather there. I paid $100 per week. I asked that the rabbi keep an eye on her. They put my sister in a room with another girl. One day she asked her roommate to have the room to herself. The Arab arrived at the hotel with a skullcap on his head. He masqueraded as a Jew. Those supervising my sister discovered him. They beat him up and threw him out.

"I got to Rabbi Meir Kahane. He told me that the Arabs are sex fiends. God gave them 90% sexual desire, and only 10% to the Jews. Kahane said that my sister had to be flown to the U.S." Eli checked out the possibility of obtaining a visa, but "they don't approve [granting a visa] to anyone who doesn't have property registered in his name in Israel," and his sister had no property. She didn't want to meet Kahane, but her brother took her to him when Kahane was leading a class in Netanya. His sister "was deeply impressed by him." After the class, they brought her to an apartment in the city. Kahane spoke with her in private. He arranged for a foster family in the United States, but she didn't want to leave Israel. Eli took out a passport for her, but she refused to sign the application for a visa.

Eli shows me all the documents.

– What now?

"Except for Kahane, there isn't a single member of Knesset who takes an interest in the issue of Arabs and Jewesses. Only one who experienced it himself knows what this is. Kahane wants to save all the Jewish girls, and not just my sister; in the meantime, however, there's no salvation. There are thousands of girls, like my sister, who go with Arabs. My sister met him on a bus in Greater Tel Aviv. He introduced himself as Avi Biton, a Jew. He's a nice fellow, may his name be blotted out. I was in his parents' house in Taibe. I threatened, but to no avail. My sister is a beautiful girl. Her Arab hates Israel. He burned cigarette holes in her [official Israeli] identity card and destroyed it. He hates the country. My sister knows that it's forbidden for her to marry him. She's very religious, and so she doesn't marry. I thought about a demonstration: to come to a party in the village, blow it up with grenades, and commit suicide."

– I heard that you take part in underground activities against Arabs.

"Nobody knows about anybody else in our movement. Every one has his own direction. Each one has an underground. Each one has his own initiative. I'm not talking about actions. Leave me alone. I won't reveal anything. You've already heard enough."

Eli is certain that Kahane will receive eight seats in the Knesset in the next elections. He wants to turn his city into a Kach bastion. "Hurt people come to Kahane, mainly those who've been hurt by Arabs, like me."

★ ★ ★

Before Kahane and his followers set out for their well-publicized expedition to Taibe, they distributed a yellow poster. In the middle of the poster is a picture of a girl, with a boy peeping behind her. The poster reads: "Miriam's children live in Bak'a el-Garbiye. These children are Jews. Their mother is a Jewess. They live in an Arab village and consider themselves Arabs. Hundreds of children like these live in Arab villages

137

today, cut off from the Jewish people. Maybe now you'll understand why we're going to the village of Taibe."

Yehuda Richter

If Meir Kahane were no longer a member of the current Knesset, or if he were to suddenly die, he would be succeeded by
Yehuda Richter, Kahane's No. 2 candidate – a convicted terrorist, currently serving a five year sentence in Tel Mond prison,
with an additional three-year suspended sentence, for attacking
Arabs.

When the last holdouts of Israel's evacuation of Sinai
threatened mass suicide – a gimmick which reaped Kahane
world-wide publicity – Richter was the "commander" of the
"suicide bunker." Of course no one committed suicide, and the
evacuation proceeded smoothly.

Richter was born in Los Angeles in 1962, and immigrated to
Israel in 1979. In March 1984 he was tried, along with Matthew
Leibowitz, Hazan Levi, and Yekutiel (Mike) Guzofsky, for
committing terrorist acts against Arabs. (A fifth member of the
group, Craig Leitner, was not indicted, after deciding to turn
state's witness; when released on bail before the end of the trial,
he fled to the United States.) All four had received training in
arms, karate, and explosives in one of the JDL's summer camps
in the United States. They knew each other in the United
States, and had participated in JDL demonstrations there before
immigrating to Israel. Richter was considered leader of the
group. Their friendship deepened in Israel, when they studied
together in yeshivot, and later during their IDF service. They
came to share a common ideology, and discussed optimal
responses to Arab terrorist attacks in Israel. They eventually
conspired to physically attack Israeli Arabs and their property.

Richter and Guzofsky, together with Leitner, were charged
with damaging Arab property in Hebron. In July 1983 they
poured gasoline under three cars in Hebron and ignited them.

The damage was estimated at 1,700 Jordanian dinars (about $4,300). They also set fire to an Arab bus in Hebron, causing $8,000-9,000 damage. The two also decided that the East Jerusalem Arab newspaper *Al-Fajr* was hostile to the State of Israel. They prepared a Molotov cocktail, and threw it into the newspaper's offices.

Levi and Richter drove around in East Jerusalem and set fire to three Arab cars in the Wadi Juz area.

Richter and Guzofsky threw homemade Molotov cocktails at the houses of Arabs in East Jerusalem, in the Shu'afat neighborhood. One firebomb exploded, and blazed away on the wall of one of the buildings.

After a terrorist attack on a bus on one of the major routes in Jerusalem, in which one young woman was killed, Leibowitz, Levi, Richter, and Leitner resolved to counter attack, i.e., to shoot at Arabs traveling in an Arab bus. Levi and Richter, who were serving in the IDF, had IDF M-16 rifles. They hid the weapons under one of the trailers used by the yeshivah in the settlement of Beit El, near Nablus. During January 1984, Richter and Leitner conducted surveillance on the bus taking Arab workers home to the village of Mazra'ah esh-Sharkiye, in the Ramallah district, and selected the site for the planned attack. Richter, the commander, designated duties: Leitner would drive the getaway car; Leibowitz – lookout and warning, providing covering fire; Richter – firing a full clip of bullets directly into the bus.

The attack was scheduled for March 4, 1984. A week earlier, Leibowitz had purchased rubber gloves and ski masks for use during the attack. He persuaded one of his friends to rent a blue Subaru for him. A day before the attack, Leibowitz and Leitner filed off the serial number of the rifle, cleaned it with alcohol to remove all fingerprints, and oiled the gun in preparation for firing. Leibowitz, Richter, and Leitner removed the rented Subaru's license plates, replacing them with plates stolen from another Subaru in Jerusalem.

They set out for the site of the ambush at 4 a.m. on March 4th. Richter loaded the M-16 with a full magazine, and hid in the site chosen for the attack. Leibowitz went to the lookout point, also carrying an M-16. His rifle was unloaded, and was meant only to intimidate. Leitner, at the wheel of the Subaru, hid in a curve in the road, out of sight of the bus, with the motor running.

The bus appeared at 5:40 a.m. Leibowitz gave Richter the order to fire, and Richter emptied the entire magazine into the bus. Six passengers were injured. The "heroes" made their escape, and hid the M-16 under some bushes in a spot they had previously chosen. When they reached Jerusalem, they discarded the ski masks and gloves in a garbage can, and put the original license plates back on the car. They discarded the stolen plates in a garbage can. They continued driving, and parked.

After the attack, Richter, Leitner, and Leibowitz hurried to Kahane, and asked him for money to pay for the rental of the Subaru. Kahane did not ask what it had been used for, and gave them $500. When they returned to where they had parked, they were arrested.

The prosecutor, Jerusalem Assistant District Attorney Michael Sheked, said that "Kahane is losing control of his people in many instances. They concealed weapons in the Kach offices. Kahane changed the locks in the office every once in a while. The accused took gasoline from Kahane's car without his knowledge. So they said. Kahane is not capable of planning such an operation. They carried it out in secret. They watched televison shows in the United States, and learned to act violently."

Leibowitz was sentenced to four years and three months imprisonment. Levi, who had participated only in the planning, but withdrew from participating in the attack itself, was sentenced to 21 months imprisonment; the government appealed the lightness of his sentence, and the Supreme Court changed his sentence to three years imprisonment, with an additional suspended sentence of two years. The Supreme Court stated in its judgement that taking the law into one's own hands and acting violently seriously harmed both the individual and society as a whole. It favored severe, deterrent sentences for the perpetrators. Guzofsky was acquitted, largely because state's witness Leitner had fled the country.

Guzofsky had also been involved in another shooting incident, together with Yisrael Fuchs, this time at Arabs in a pickup in the Hebron hills. Fuchs, who was eventually deported from Israel, met a leading figure in Kach who was in prison at the time. The Kach leader (who is no longer affiliated with the movement) told me that Fuchs named Kahane as being responsible for the burning and destruction of the Baptist church in Jerusalem. He said, "I understood from the conversation with Fuchs that Rabbi Kahane was in the picture."

Richter's statements during his trial reveal much of his personality. He launched into a long, rambling, semicoherent discourse on recent Zionist and Jewish history, in an attempt to justify his actions. The monologue was finally halted by Richter's own attorney, who lost patience with his client. The presiding judge noted that he would have interrupted Richter had the prosecutor requested it. After his lawyer instructed him to get to the point, Richter said that "Violence is very bad, but at times, in order to rescue the Jewish people, there is no alternative. You should know that no one from the Irgun Tzva'i Leumi wanted to carry out actions like these. Everyone wanted peace. Therefore they did what they did for lack of an alternative, in order to insure that the next generation would not have to be faced with such a choice, but gentlemen, the current generation, to our sorrow, has reached the end of the road. All of your assumptions are correct. There is an obligation to maintain the law. OK, and an individual is forbidden to take away the government's authority, but can we be content with this; perhaps there is another side to the coin?..."

Judge Noam responded, "There is a government in this country, and it decides, and you do not decide..."; the judge rejected as irrelevant Richter's reference to an increase in the rate of growth of the Arab population, and his "prayer that the government of Israel would begin to deal harshly with Arab inciters." Richter interjected "You should know that I acted out of love of Israel, and not out of hatred for the Arabs, whom I really understand." He added that he had rejected an offer to drop the charges against him in return for agreeing to be expelled from the country; he explained to the authorities that "I will

141

stay in Israel for good or bad. In the meantime, I pray and anticipate, every day, only that true peace will arrive."

Richter's arguments convinced neither the prosecutor nor the judge. The prosecutor found it "difficult to accept that the defendant meant only to intimidate the Arabs when he faced a bus full of workers and emptied the magazine of an M-16 rifle into it, not at the wheels and not in the air, but, into the windshield at the height of the driver's head." He also rejected Richter's claim that this act was in opposition to his true nature. The prosecutor concluded by reminding the court that Richter was the No. 2 candidate on Kach's Knesset list, and that his acts showed that his nature and character were consistent with "a war to the bitter end against the Arabs, every end justifies the means, and the law does not exist."

The verdict was delivered in Jerusalem District Court on November 9, 1984. Judge Noam stated in his verdict that the "court was commanded to warn of the seriousness [of the crime] and to deter with fitting punishments, with the goal of uprooting the evil."

If Kach had received only a few more votes, Yehuda Richter would have become a member of the Eleventh Knesset, and would have enjoyed parliamentary immunity.

Gad Servetman

The grandfather was a member of the pioneering "Labor Battalions" that engaged in physical work (draining swamps, building roads, etc.) to build the renewed Jewish homeland in the 1920's. The grandson, Gad Servetman, is the current Kach spokesman. He was born in 1959 in Tel Aviv, and grew up in Kfar Saba. He served in the Israeli Air Force as an airplane electrician. He moved to Kiryat Arba, and studied in its yeshivah for eight months in 1980. He later moved to the Old City in Jerusalem. His parents, who are nonreligious, divorced when Gad was five years old. His membership in the Gesher youth movement, which attempts to build bridges between the religious and nonreligious, introduced him to the concepts of Judaism. He was already religious by the time he served in the Air Force.

He joined Kach in 1976 after reading a newspaper advertisement. In 1977 he was an unimportant Kach functionary in Bnei Brak. By the 1981 elections he already was a leading activist in the movement. After the elections he heeded the call of Rabbi Yisrael Ariel, the No. 2 Kach candidate in 1981, and went to Ophira in the Sinai Peninsula for the founding of the Gevul Yisrael yeshivah.

Servetman claims that his activities against Arabs are "a function of my activity for Jews." He cites Rakah MK Tawfiq Zayyad as an example of Arabs being "against" Jews, and asks me if I know the poem which Zayyad read in the Knesset after the Yom Kippur War, and which "praised the slaughterers of the Jews."

He believes that Arabs "don't want" Jews in Israel. When asked why Kach went to Um el-Fahum, and what the Kach activists wanted to do in the Arab village, he replies, "We intended to take a walk in the streets of the village, to take a trip in the great outdoors. Why are Arabs permitted to walk in the streets of Tiberias?"

Servetman and the Kach leadership have only one goal: "To remove the Arabs from the Land of Israel, if not in a good spirit, then in a not-good spirit." He asks, "Won't the government, which succeeded in removing thousands of Jews from Yamit, succeed in removing a few Arabs?" He's generous. "We'll give them an option: to leave with compensation." He's convinced that the government will decide upon this course of action sooner or later, passing a law to this effect. He admits that this is not realistic today, but believes that when Kach has 10 or 16 representatives in the Knesset ("This will be the situation in the Thirteenth Knesset"), the movement will be asked to join the government.

Servetman rejects the charge that Kach is composed of madmen, or people on the fringe of society, and maintains that the idea of removing the Arabs from Israel is supported by

Minister Gideon Patt, Likud MK Meir Cohen-Avidov, and Maj.-Gen. Yanush Ben Gal. He also cites past support for the idea by Labor party ideologue Berl Katzenelson and author Hayim Hazaz.

– What is behind the transfer plan?

"Our goal is to establish a Jewish state here in accordance with Jewish religious law."

– What will happen to the minorities living in the country?

"They won't live here any more."

– What would happen if non-Jews behaved this way towards Jews in the Diaspora?

"If only this were so. This would lead to the removal of the Jews from the Diaspora and their immigration to Israel. We'll pay them, just so they'll immigrate here, but they will immigrate only when it will be bad for them in the Diaspora."

There is no internal democracy within Kach, and it has no elected bodies. Servetman says that Kahane "consults" with those close to him (who change with dizzying rapidity). He explains the constant changes in the leadership of Kach by mentioning "the difficulty of people to continue with Kahane.... They don't last because Kahane is charismatic and overshadows everyone." When we discuss various personality clashes within the Kach leadership, Servetman admits that the movement was "on the brink of disintegrating on the eve of the 1984 Knesset elections. If we hadn't gotten to the Knesset, who knows what fate would have befallen the movement." In contrast, "Now we have recognition, a base, a starting point. There is also the beginning to the top, a new stage which will permit continuity. We were ostracized before, but now we have immunity."

Servetman lists those currently close to Kahane; one of them, Kach Knesset faction secretary Baruch Marzel, was arrested on March 30, 1985, on suspicion of firing on the house of a released Arab terrorist and of participating in the intimidation and harassment of terrorists released in exchange for Israeli POW's. Servetman says the Kach leadership meets once a week to discuss current operations. When Kahane decides to take a certain action, he listens to activists in the field and consults with them. Kahane generally conceives and initiates the plan himself. The

144

details are then worked out with those implementing it. (All evidence contradicts Servetman's description.)

Servetman confirmed Kach's utilization of the serious economic situation and growing unemployment in Israel, as well as increasing antagonism towards Arabs. "There already is a certain fear among the Arabs. They sense that Kahane is a rising power, and that the public buys his ideas. When unemployment deepens, with the Jew not working, and the Arab working, they will turn to Kahane. If we have five or six seats in the Knesset, they will need Kahane as a [government] minister, the Arabs will understand what awaits them. If we had two Knesset seats today, one of them at the expense of the Alignment, the Likud would chase after Kahane, woo him fervently. If Kahane will be Defense Minister in another 20 years, the Arabs will certainly want to leave Israel."

– Then why don't you wait 20 years? Why all the provocations and incitement now?

"In the meantime, [we're] causing disturbances. This is very important, so that the public will know who the Arab really is. This counterfeit Jewish-Arab coexistence won't exist. This is a balloon which must be burst. It's all air. A little stab with a knife and all the air goes out.

– What about economic problems?

"I don't know if economics – bread – is indeed the main issue. The Arab is the existential issue. What difference does it make if the devaluation will increase or be halted? The economy is No. 2 on the list of priorities."

When I mention that Kach is ostracized by everyone today, Servetman insists "the reason for this is simple: what Rabbi Kahane says today, the others will say tomorrow." To bolster his vision, he claims that Kahane's pronouncements on the need to settle Kiryat Arba preceded Moshe Levinger, and that Levinger opposed Kahane on this issue then. "They don't like him because he's a prophet of doom. Today, it's more and more clear that he's right. Kahane and Levinger danced together in the Simhat Torah celebrations in Hebron in October 1984. Minister Ariel Sharon also danced with him."

– Kahane's teachings remind one of Khomeini's teachings in

Iran, and Hitler's racial laws.

"So what? So what if there isn't any difference? What's it any of our business? We are Jews, and we'll go according to Judaism, and we won't check, or compare, if there is or isn't any resemblance to Khomeini's teachings. I don't agree with your determination of the facts."

– Kahane repeatedly claims that the Holocaust was caused by the Jews' not observing the Torah. Can such a claim be made at the end of the 20th century?

"If the Jewish people had done what the Torah commands it to do – to immigrate to Israel – there would have been no Holocaust. This is the basis and foundation of Israel's Torah: immigration to Israel."

Kahane labels all his critics with the derogatory terms "defeatists" and "Hellenists." How can this be justified in a pluralistic society, in which everyone has his own opinions?

"Kahane has the right to call whoever he wants a defeatist or Hellenist. All those who introduce non-Jewish values into Israel, such as shouting when a terrorist who attacked a girl soldier is killed, but – remaining silent about the attack on the soldier; or those who bring Western culture, like a Rod Stewart concert, where they faint during the performance. These are Hellenists. Look how they go in the street and how they look: a ring in the ear, long hair, sloppy clothes. This is Hellenism – and Greece was once the center of culture."

– Who among you gives the orders to set out on actions, on special operations, mainly against Arabs?

"Rabbi Kahane approves when there are instances which require action, such as separating a Jewess and an Arab. I won't go into details because this is liable to cause harm. He approves the distribution of fliers in Arab cities in the middle of the night, in secret. The fliers are written in Hebrew. I won't talk about actions to separate Arabs from Jewesses."

– Why didn't you express sorrow at the death of Emil Grunsweig of Peace Now?

"There are Jews who should be mourned more than Emil Grunsweig. Don't forget that he was active in a movement that acts against the Jewish people. The dozens of Jews who were

146

murdered by terrorists should be mourned more than Grunsweig. Those who speak against political terror have no right to do so. Their predecessors attacked the *Altalena*, made the *Saison*, spread libels about Arlosoroff." [Servetman refers to three instances of attacks on Revisionists by the predecessors of today's Alignment; these instances are frequently cited by Revisionists and their successors as examples of left-wing persecution. The *Altalena* was an Irgun Tzva'i Leumi ship bringing arms and immigrants to Israel in 1948, and was fired upon by the Palmach, which was identified politically with the left; the *Saison* refers to the period in 1944-45 when the Hagana handed over Irgun Tzva'i Leumi and Lehi (the "Stern Gang") members to the British Mandatory authorities; Revisionists were accused of having murdered Hayim Arlosoroff, the head of the Political Section of the Jewish Agency – trans.]

– You want to expel all the Arabs. Does this also include the Druze? Kahane was forced to apologize to the Druze, after having sent them letters calling on them to immigrate.

"Sending letters to the Druze to leave Israel was a mistake. Kahane did not intend to write to them. In the final analysis, however, they will have to leave also, since Israel is meant only for Jews."

In the 1984 elections Gad Servetman was No. 12 on the Kach list. If he maintains his position in Kach, he will occupy a higher place on the list in the next elections. Yoel Lerner, who has served much time in Israeli jails for terrorist activities, said that "Kahane is a dove in comparison with him [Servetman]. I don't feel comfortable with him. He's very extreme."

Former Disciples

Kahane's former followers – even former leaders of his organizations – speak of him in a different tone. Almost all have parted ways with their former leader and associate. Some say they still agree with Kahane's ideas, but can no longer work with him because of his loner personality. Others have become his sworn enemies. Bertram Zweibon, one of the co-founders of the Jewish Defense League, told me at the end of 1984 that he had made Kahane, and he would break him.

The accusations tumble out, one after another. Kahane's diatribes are about Jewish women living with Arab men, yet not once has he ever attacked Jewish men who live with Arab women. Why hasn't he?

He constantly preaches on the need to establish a state based on Jewish law, yet, for some reason, he would not be willing to accept the authority of the greatest rabbis, or of any rabbi.

Then again, Kahane constantly harps on how poor he is, how he only has the one suit he's wearing, and that is years old. Yet the man is a thief. He has stolen money given to the League and used it for his own purposes. "He's an egomaniac. He's a megalomaniac."

Why did it take Zweibon so long to realize whom he was dealing with? He explains it was a long, drawn-out process. Whereas in 1973 Kahane had sent out directives from Israel to the United States to have the JDL attack Soviet diplomats, by 1984 was calling in the Jewish Press for the murder of Jews. That was the last straw – calling for the assassination of Jews who disagree with his policies. Now he feels that Kahane is a clear menace to Israel, the Jews and Jewish law, and he has chosen no longer to remain silent.

Morton Dolinsky, the third founder of JDL, gave an interview to a United Press reporter a week after assuming the position of director of the Israeli Government Press Office, in which he strongly criticized Kahane's plan to expel the Arabs from Israel (in response, Dolinsky received a telegram from "Josh Landau, chairman of the Friends of Kahane," threatening that "now that we've attained several elements of power, we plan to deal with you as you've dealt with us.")

The most interesting attitude towards Kahane by a former associate is undoubtedly Yoel Lerner's. Lerner has impeccable right-wing terrorist credentials: he has spent most of the past decade in and out of Israeli jails on charges of conspiracy, possessing arms without a license, conducting underground military training, and conspiring to plant a bomb next to the Dome of the Rock on the Temple Mount. Lerner wants to establish a state based on Jewish religious law in Israel. As part of this proposed state, he would expel all Christians from Israel. He declines, "on the advice of my lawyer," to say whether he plans to achieve this goal by democratic means. Lerner accepts Kahane's ideology, but says he differs from Kahane in that. Kahane speaks of the expulsion of the Arabs, which Lerner views as only one facet of his ideal Jewish religious state. Although he differs from Kahane on tactics, Lerner voted for Kahane four times. Yet even when Lerner was actively involved in the organization, he was aware of Kahane's darker side. During the 1973 elections Lerner realized that there was a large gap between Kahane's words and his actions. Lerner told me that Kahane does everything for media coverage. "It is possible that he is pathological in his publicity seeking, but he also has certain ideological lines. It is possible that he wants both to get his message across and to win publicity." More seriously, Lerner took care not to inform Kahane of operational plans, because he knew that his leader would run to inform the Security Services. On one occasion, Lerner and another activist planned the kidnapping of the Norwegian ambassador to Israel, to hold him as hostage until the release of the Israeli security agents who were captured after shooting an Arab in Lillehammer under the misconception he was a leading Arab terrorist. Lerner requested organizational assistance from Yossi Schneider, the director-general of Kach at the time. When Lerner and his associate discovered that Schneider had told Kahane of the plan, Lerner quickly cancelled it. (Yossi Schneider confirmed this, stating, "I told Kahane, and Lerner quickly cancelled the plan.")

20

Kahane's Lawyers

Rahamim Cohen

Significantly, of all Kahane's former associates, only his lawyers have a good word to say for him. Rahamim Cohen was one of Kahane's first lawyers in Israel. In 1977 he occupied the No. 3 position on the Kach list. Born in Bulgaria in 1939, Cohen came to Israel at the age of eight. He is married and the father of three children. In 1983 he was appointed to the prestigious position of legal counsel for Mekorot, the national water corporation.

Cohen's flirtation with Kahane began on a professional basis. Kahane was involved in several trials, and someone recommended Cohen. The two met after Kahane's trial in the arms-smuggling affair which involved Amihai Paglin. Cohen's background suited Kahane: right-wing views, membership in Betar in high school. Cohen was disappointed by Herut, which he claimed had "become moderate, bourgeois, and establishment, long before the political 'upheaval' of 1977" (in which the Likud, with Herut as its central component, came to power). Cohen viewed Kahane as the true heir to the philosophy of Betar. Cohen joined the Jewish Defense League, and occupied a central role in the JDL by the 1977 elections. His activity in the movement centered on propaganda, together with the legal services he provided. Kahane had difficulty in paying his legal costs. Cohen, who said that Kahane paid "as much as he could," viewed his legal services as his contribution to the movement.

From the outset of his involvement with Kach, Cohen heard criticism of Kahane by his closest associates. They wanted Kahane to present his views in a balanced, moderate fashion, but Kahane ignored them. Cohen justifies Kahane's pursuit of headlines, remarking "there is no greater justification than success." Cohen cites the example of Lova Eliav, who ran on his own ticket and did not enter the 11th Knesset. Cohen says that "there is no disputing his [Eliav's] rights and qualities," but points out that Eliav was unsuccessful in mobilizing electoral strength "because of the clean campaign which he waged."

Cohen defends Kahane's violent methods, stating that in today's sorry state of affairs, "there's no other way of entering the Knesset than descending to the sewers, otherwise you don't make it to parliament; in a democracy, everything is determined by quantity and not quality, and the vote of an illiterate is equal to that of an educated person." He finds nothing wrong with Kahane's tactics, "because the operative conclusions are the same, whether you present them in an inciting manner, or through logical persuasion. The logical conclusion in either case is that the Arabs must be forcibly expelled from the Land of Israel."

Cohen speaks fluently, forcefully. He is not ashamed of his philosophy, and does not ask to hide behind a screen of anonymity, as did many of the other people I inteviewed while writing this book. He assesses events soberly. "In today's reality, you can't act this way with Arabs, but this is the goal towards which we must aspire, just as the socialist parties aspire towards their goal of establishing a socialist society."

Cohen has no doubts concerning the realistic chances of such a "solution" to the Arab problem. Well-versed in the pronouncements by Mapai leaders encouraging Arab emigration during the War of Independence, he envisages a population exchange within the context of peace treaties, and optimistically thinks it within reach. He believes that a portion of the Arabs would be ready to leave willingly; the rest "would have to be forced." In his view, this will happen sooner than the Arabs think, because the Arab minority "will turn our lives into a hell, worsening each and every day: sabotage, subversion, prolonged rebellion, disturbing everyday life."

He strongly attacks the "bleeding hearts," finding them "extremely hypocritical." He charges that "It is easy for them to say that the Arabs don't bother us – but those saying so live in wealth and comfort in Savyon, Afeka, Tel Baruch, northern Tel Aviv [all wealthy areas]; you won't hear this from the inhabitants of Upper Nazareth, Jaffa, Acre, places where Jews and Arabs live in close proximity. The process will be stopped only by the drastic method of expulsion."

Cohen has a ready answer about the feasibility of such a step in a democratic State with the eyes of the world focused on it. "First you cut the benefits granted to Arabs. They benefit from National Insurance, but don't serve in the IDF. Places in universities are reserved for them. Laws must be enacted against benefits to Arabs." As for the world's reaction, "People don't act in our world according to sentimental considerations, but rather according to cynical interest. If they respond – for us or against us – they will do this, not necessarily as a consequence of actions which were taken, but according to utilitarian interests. Most countries in the world support the USSR despite its disgusting acts at every moment, in every place. This is due to the interest of the countries which support Moscow. They will act in the same manner concerning us. On the other hand, the Biafrans were exterminated despite the sympathy which they received from the world.... Policy cannot be conducted according to considerations of the future."

According to Cohen, since no steps have been taken on the transfer, it cannot be determined ahead of time that the expulsion will not succeed. He emphasizes that everything is being done in the opposite direction. The Arabs are encouraged by the benefits lavished upon them; they respond with hatred. Cohen maintains that it will not be possible to buy the Arabs, even if endless economic benefits are showered on them. Israel cannot escape from the problem; accordingly a realistic path, that of persuading as many voters as possible that Rabbi Kahane's way is the right one, must be adopted. Kahane's electoral success in 1984 is "a result of the specific reality of increasing extremism between Jews and Arabs." He is certain that Kahane's strength will increase, and that he will assume power in Israel. He draws an analogy between Kahane and Menahem Begin, who was a pariah for many years, but finally became prime minister. Kahane won't wait as long as Begin. Cohen admits that Kahane has many negative qualities, but even so is capable of leading a movement that will take power in Israel.

He paints the following scenario: "Kahane will find the right people by his side as the number of his supporters increases. It is an illusion to think that Kahane will disappear if the government adopts a stronger policy in the territories. The problem is too profound to be solved by intensifying the measures used in the territories. There is a conflict here between two peoples, and there is no just solution for both of them. The stronger will win."

When asked to explain why he is no longer active in Kach, he prefaces his reply by remarking that "quality people" do not fit into Kahane's organization. Cohen adds that the specific reason why he left Kach is because his position in Mekorot, a public corporation, does not permit him to be active in Kach; he has not, however, changed his views.

Cohen admits that there are marginal characters in Kach, but these of all people "have a healthier political intuition than do the bleeding hearts, the educated, and the intellectuals." These marginal types intuitively arrive at more correct solutions than the "brainy types."

– Aren't these solutions racial laws, like those of Hitler?

"I'm not bothered by [the charge of] Hitler's laws. The Jewish people was faithful all through the years to maintain its existence; therefore we oppose intermarriage, but not conversion. Therefore I justify Kahane's demand to enact legislation against intermarriage. This is one of the ancient Jewish principles, from Israel's Torah. We are commanded to [maintain] a pure race. The Jewish people is unique. We must not assimilate among other peoples. We are 'a people that dwells apart' [Num. 23:9]."

He explains that even the secular Bulgarian Jewish community fanatically maintained Jewish racial purity in the Diaspora; how is it possible that in Israel, of all places, we will cast this aside? He admits that there is an opposing viewpoint, which permits intermarriage, but this will lead to assimilation: "Whoever thinks that it is preferable for the Jewish people to assimilate and be wiped out, as happened to all the ancient peoples, will not see anything wrong with mixed marriages, but whoever desires the continued existence of the Jewish people will agree with Kahane."

There is no middle path for Cohen. He himself is nationalist-secular, but Kahane convinced him that the philosophy of religious coercion is correct. He states that "the madness of secular nationalism has no justification. If you do not believe, the conclusion is to assimilate, and then no Jews will remain in Israel." He himself is not personally observant, but he does believe in the existence of Divine Providence, and that Israel has a mission, with Divine Providence dictating Israel's fate. He agrees with Kahane's vision of a state run in accordance with Jewish religious law. When pressed, he agrees that his position, theoretically, would not be very comfortable. He states that "The nonobservance of the commandments is indeed a fault in my education, but I would do everything in order to adapt myself to such a way of life in a religious state; I will correct this fault, recognizing that Judaism guards the existence of the people.... I believe that Jewish law developed during the course of time, and can certainly also serve the needs of modern man."

Cohen, the True Believer, states emphatically that "the reality of a religious state is realistic, and close at hand."

Rahamim Cohen, a lawyer, with a broad education, holding an important public post, admits that Kahane's ideas attract many strange people, "but this does not mean his ideas are faulty. As an individual, he possesses the most impressive personality I've ever met. He possesses extraordinary intelligence and has both feet firmly on the ground.... He's very realistic. He has an extraordinary sense for the media. He's in the headlines every day, despite the decision to place him under a media ban. This reminds me of movie stars: they don't care

154

what is written about them, just so long as something is written. I've never met anyone with so refined a character as Kahane. He's the opposite of his external, violent cover. His conduct is a tactic to win headlines. He isn't capable of harming an Arab, not even a fly. He isn't violent."

The rabbi is also a miracle worker. Cohen relates that he and his wife had a friend who almost went blind. Kahane came to the Cohen family to encourage their friend. He promised to pray for her at the Western Wall, and did. After an operation performed in Israel failed, Kahane gave her the address of a doctor in the United States who would take care of her. She went to the United States, and her sight was saved in an operation there. The conclusions which Cohen draws from this episode border on superstition: "This isn't a fairy tale. This testifies to the quality of the man. Kahane says that in the world in which we live, where people aren't willing to let someone cut into line, and are willing to kill for a penny, they are willing to give up the heritage of the Patriarchs without blinking an eyelash. This is the cause of the gap between the personal conduct of each individual in everyday life and his conduct in the national sphere.

"He has a sense of humor. He is honest, and poor as well. He has many fields of interest. Literature. Poetry. Sport. He himself played basketball. He has no equal as a man of faith; he doesn't just pay lip service. I represented him when he was under administrative detention in Ramle Prison in the summer of 1980. The evidence was secret, but rumor had it that he had been arrested in connection with having conspired to attack the Temple Mount. This was an absolute lie, an excuse to neutralize him by Ezer Weizman, who was defense minister then. I visited Kahane in Ramle Prison. He told me that he was suffering from disappointment and frustration. He asked, 'For whom am I laboring?' He told me, 'I'm sitting in jail, and the Jewish people doesn't care, but what encourages me? When I see the PLO people here in the prison, they are human beings too, and they have families, and they too are cut off, but they are happy and lighthearted [Kahane makes frequent use of Biblical language; see Esther 5:9 – trans.], with high morale, because they are

155

strengthened by their belief and ideology. Can I possibly be weaker than they are?..."

– How can you support someone like Kahane, who encourages violence, cooperates with the secret services, and even handed over Amihai Paglin to the authorities?

Cohen is not excited by the question. He replies, "In my opinion and estimation, illegal acts were never done in the movement under the guidance of Kahane or with his knowledge; after the fact, however, he grants ideological support to actions and operations, understanding their motives. It is true that Amihai Paglin accused Kahane of being an informer. There is always somebody from the General Security Services planted among us. For the most part, the plants were among the most dedicated activists, who served the movement well. We don't care. We were within the realm of legitimate activity. Kahane's claim is that a party cannot be an underground. But if others make an underground – with our blessings."

Cohen told me that he was witness in 1980 to a meeting held in his office between Kahane and one of Israel's leading businessmen. The businessman was of the opinion that propaganda, fliers, and mere words were insufficient; he wanted to finance actual underground activities against Arabs. According to Cohen, Kahane totally rejected the businessman's offer. Cohen said, "Kahane isn't an idiot. He is realistic. He's aware of the fact that he is a well-known figure, and is under surveillance. Underground activity might completely neutralize him. He's a soloist, and doesn't accept advice. He does what he thinks is correct. In intimate meetings with his people he doesn't enforce his opinion, and seems to accept the majority opinion, but a day or two later he'll act in his own way. This is not expressed in a confrontation, but in a lack of regard for the other people and their views. He does what he alone wants to do."

Cohen reels off the names of those who were, or are, close to Kahane: Yossi Dayan, Yossi Shneider, Yoel Lerner, Avigdor Eskin, Moshe Potolsky. "They're individualists." When I mention that all of them, except for Potolsky (No. 2 on the Kach list in the 1977 elections), have left Kahane, Cohen replies that the phenomenon of individualists coming and going is also

156

characteristic of the Israeli left. He praised Eli Adir, the Kach director-general at the time of the interview; a few months later, Adir also left Kahane, referring to his erstwhile idol as "a dictator; impulsive; moody; blind to reality – sometimes like Don Quixote; always referring to himself as the only righteous man alive, and all others as erring. On many occasions he is ruled by his emotions. He doesn't consult with anyone..."

Meir Shechter.

Meir Shechter is a different type altogether. A member of the Morasha party, he was active in the religious Poalei Agudat Yisrael party. He wears a small knitted skullcap. He is a pleasant conversationalist, open, and critical as well. When I spoke with him, at the end of 1984 and the beginning of 1985, the 40-year-old lawyer was kept busy by his old client Kahane. Kahane was filing appeals by the dozen to the High Court of Justice whenever someone infringed on his rights as a member of Knesset. The two have worked together since October 1971, when Kahane set up his first office in the prestigious Rehavia quarter of Jerusalem, retaining Shechter as his lawyer. He stopped representing Kahane a few years ago, and Kahane was represented by Leorit Daniel. In 1982 Kahane returned to Shechter. There is a chemistry between the two.

Shechter basically agrees with Kahane's teachings. They see eye to eye on religious matters. Unlike Kahane, however, Shechter was born in Israel, is part of the Israeli reality, and does not live in a dreamworld. Shechter agrees that some of Kahane's ideas are extremely superficial. Thinking aloud, he says Kahane's national-Jewish ideology may be correct, but it cannot be reconciled with normative government in Israel, nor with the law of the land; it is doubtful whether he will ever be able to implement it. Kahane will never subordinate his ideological beliefs to secular laws enacted by the Knesset. According to Shechter, his client Kahane is a political innocent, who shows no signs of maturing. This is borne out by the young age of Kahane's supporters. He finds Kahane "an extremely interesting conversationalist." He asserts that Kahane is also a very talented and prolific writer, and a master at manipulating the media. The 1984 campaign clearly shows this: the voter heard and read mainly about three candidates: Shimeon Peres, Yitzhak Shamir, and Meir Kahane. Kahane ran for the Knesset so that he would have a platform from which "to shout," to disseminate his ideas and to attempt to implement them.

Responding to the charge that Kahane is a racist, Shechter notes that if Kahane is a racist, so is the Bible, but this is not so. Racism implies the existence of a closed-off superior race, like the Aryans as conceived by Hitler. This is not the case with Jews. Any non-Jew can convert, join the people, and even become a chief rabbi; there were rabbis who were converts. Kahane wants a Jewish state without non-Jews, who endanger its existence and Jewish character. The Declaration of Independence is a universal, not a Jewish document, and is internally inconsistent. On the one hand, it proclaims the establishment of the Jewish state, and on the other, provides full equality for all. If so, then how does one maintain the Jewish majority? We have to do what Kahane says: granting second-class rights to the Arabs, denying the right to vote in elections to the Knesset. What the world thinks is not important. An Arab who doesn't like such an arrangement can go to an Arab country.

Shechter compares Kahane to a horse with blinders. He is pessimistic about Kahane's future in Israel. He points out that his philosophy can make news, but will not be accepted. Kahane will not get more than four seats in the Knesset in the next fifteen years. Kach is a one-man movement. Kahane has the power to influence the young. He arouses the Sephardim, and revives their pride, telling them, "You are the real Jews, you were deprived all these years, all your lives; you are as good as the Ashkenazim. You know how dangerous the Arabs are, since you lived with them." He also has a common language with the Americans in his group, most of whom are religious, many newly so. They know that anti-Semitism is apt to increase in their native countries. Kahane proposes preventive medicine, telling them to immigrate to Israel. He proposes an alternative for those staying in the United States – activity in the JDL. He tells them to be men and set up defense organizations.

Shechter says what many people think: Kahane's chances of increasing his strength are dependent on the extent of terrorist attacks and future wars in Israel. Without these, he will disappear from the political map. Shechter says that everyone thinks like Kahane, but does not talk like him, since they understand that they must reconcile themselves to the current situation living with Arabs. We are living in the twentieth century; there are not two classes of citizens in the world, and the fate and status of Diaspora Jewry must be taken into account.

– Why doesn't an intelligent lawyer like Shechter bring Kahane closer to his own views?

"Kahane is the one who imposes his views on others," replies Shechter, almost in a whisper. Kahane's lawyers must agree with him, or at least agree to represent his opinions. Shechter describes Kahane as extremely nervous, wound up like a spring all the time. He's emotional, someone who never sheds a tear, a strong man who can't be broken. Since he's been ostracized by the establishment, the media is the only avenue left for him to express himself, and he has to do extraordinary actions to get to the media. He succeeds in getting on the news and in appearing on television by means of his extreme actions, such as in Um el-Fahum. The continual tension which he is under, and the fact that he is constantly in a defensive position leads to signs of never-ending nervousness. Other people have to adapt themselves to him. To some degree, he can be ignited by a provocation. He's aware of this. Provocative questions annoy him. He's not a person to make friends in society. He doesn't have supporters among the establishment religious community.

– Why is this so?

Kahane speaks in the name of Jewish law, and says things which make many people hate Judaism. There is also another aspect to the problem: as the late Chief Ashkenazi Rabbi, Yitzhak Levi Herzog, said, "In the conditions in which we find ourselves in the world, it is forbidden to expel the Arabs from the Land of Israel."

Shechter is full of praise for Kahane, even when others are not. He says that Kahane cares, almost like a father, for his people. Kahane calls Shechter day or night whenever someone is arrested. He's the first to visit his people in prison. He lives like a monk. His clothes are few and old. The tension caused by his failures in the past, and his lack of acceptance by those whom he would expect to be sympathetic (the right, Gush Emunim, the Tehiya party), is noticeable on his face.

When I remarked that Shechter's positive evaluation of Kahane is contradicted by all my other research, and by those who were close to Kahane in the past, he replied only that Kahane "has almost no personal shortcomings. You can rely on his word. Respect for his fellow-man. You can rely on him blindly." When I pressed Shechter, he added, "Rabbi Moshe Levinger, the leader of Gush Emunim, presents his ideas in a rational manner, but Kahane presents his ideas in a nonrational manner, which drives people away from him. He's extremely knowledgeable. The Bible never leaves his hand. If he has to wait, he'll study the Bible. When he was imprisoned he read and wrote books on Judaism." About Kahane's calling his critics "Hellenists" [historically, the purveyors of Greek culture and the opponents of the Maccabees in the struggle commemorated by the Hannukah holiday], Shechter comments, "Anyone whose opinion contradicts the Torah is a Hellenist in Kahane's eyes."

Leorit Daniel.

Leorit Daniel's connection with Kach began in 1978, when Rahamim Cohen asked her to defend Yossi Dayan, the Kach director-general at the time, who was charged with violent activities. She also defended Allan Goodman, who had fired shots on the Temple Mount. Goodman was not a member of Kach, but Kahane hurried to finance his defense. Goodman, a paranoid-schizophrenic, punched Daniel in the face when he suspected her of having told his mother of his behavior.

(According to sources in the United States, Goodman had been a member of the JDL at least two years before the incident on the Temple Mount, and had trained in one of the JDL's camps near Harrison, New York.)

Daniel characterized Kach as "a fluid movement. They have diffculty in mobilizing five people for a demonstration. He [Kahane] was elected to the Knesset because people became more extreme. Kach acted all these years by mobilizing people on an *ad hoc* basis for demonstrations. It's easy for anyone who doesn't have real answers to the question of the Arabs to be swept away by Kahane. Kahane says out loud what others think to themselves. He increases and deepens hatred towards the Arabs. All the latent Kahanism is coming out. If he were more serious, he would reap more success. The journalistic coverage of him is indeed anti, but even this excites his followers. It brings him votes. Kahane is a one-man party. [His] No. 2 is Yehudah Richter, who's in prison. On the eve of the elections we wanted to film him in Tel Mond Prison for political advertisements on television. We filed an appeal to the High Court of Justice, but the court session was set for the day after the last political advertisements were broadcast."

I asked Daniel, who is a leading activist in the Association of Civil Rights in Israel, whether Kahane is a racist. "This is a complicated question. He doesn't possess any racist attitudes. He has a proposal for ordering the problem with the Arabs: the status of resident alien. He wants a law which will establish a prohibition on sexual relations between Jews and Arabs, and also to revoke their right to vote and to be elected. We can say that this is the norm of a country, to defend itself by preventing an Arab majority. Is this racism? There is a serious difficulty in establishing a definition of racism, for fear of limiting freedom of expression. Kahane claims he speaks the truth, and does not incite. He was elected on his 'racist' platform; if there were a law against racism, it would be necessary to revoke his [parliamentary] immunity in order to put him on trial. Revoking his immunity is inconceivable, because of the connection between his immunity and the things which he preaches and his platform; he does not deviate from the platform on which he was legally elected."

Daniel notes that the ACRI requested all members of Knesset to sign a petition censuring the expulsion of Arabs, "but only a few signed."

– How do we fight against Kahane?

"You can't silence him in the media. You have to contend with him. Answers have to be given to the questions which he raises in public. If there are no answers to the issues he raises, the problems become more severe. Professor Yishayahu Leibowitz claims the Alignment is the source of Kahane. I have a problem: on the one hand, I don't want to restrict anyone like Kahane from speaking, because of the need to contend with the phenomenon and the desire to protect freedom of expression; on the other hand, I don't want a legislator like Kahane in the Knesset."

Daniel conducted a study of the legal aspects of the Kach movement. She discovered that the courts treated the movement leniently, thereby providing approval for violations of the law, after the fact turning violence into a legitimate means of attaining the political, religious, and other goals of Kahane's hooligans. If Kahane and his people had received the stiff penalties called for by pertinent laws, it is possible that Kahane would have spent his time studying the Bible in Israeli prisons, rather than being elected to the Knesset. A few examples suffice:

The Cave of Mahpelah: At the end of 1978 Yossi Dayan and the more violent members of Kach were tried by a military court in Hebron. Kiryat Arba residents were not satisfied with the regulations limiting times and locations of prayer by Jews within the Cave. Jews began to violate the regulations; Arabs grew agitated, and there was danger of disturbances. The military administration issued orders restricting entry to the cave by Dayan and a number of other Kach leaders. Dayan violated the order, entering the cave on January 20, 1979. He later fled from legal custody and twice interfered with soldiers carrying out their orders. The law provides for a maximum penalty of 5 years imprisonment for each of these crimes. Dayan could have been sentenced to a total of 20 years in prison. He was sentenced to two weeks imprisonment (less the time he had already spent in detention), a three-month suspended sentence, and a small fine of IL 2,000. Even this ridiculously lenient sentence was not implemented. Dayan appealed for a pardon from the commander of the Judea and Samaria region, who granted it.

The Avraham Avinu Synagogue: This synagogue is located in the heart of Hebron, next to the marketplace. The building was abandoned and neglected. At the end of 1978, Kiryat Arba residents, including Kach activists, began to create "facts on the ground" at the site, in order to force the authorities to renovate the building and restore its function as a synagogue. An order issued by the Hebron military governor declared the site a closed area. On October 18, 1978, Dayan and a dozen others, including Ze'ev Friedman, head of the Kiryat Arba administration, entered the closed area and attacked the soldiers who attempted to remove them. Each crime carried a 5-year maximum sentence, a total of 15 years imprisonment in all. Two defendants were acquitted of all charges. Dayan was found guilty on two counts, after having been acquitted on the charge of refusing to leave a closed area. He received a six-month suspended sentence and was fined IL 1,000.

The Temple Mount: The Temple Mount was always a focal point for violent activity by Kahane and his followers. After a violent incident at the end of March 1979, all participants, except Kahane and Dayan, were charged with trespassing, malicious assault, threats, insults to religion, and other crimes. After a deal with the prosecution, the defendants received sentences of 23 days in jail, with an additional suspended sentence of six months. In other words, the defendants were released immediately after the trial. In all these cases, as well as in an incident involving trespassing and illegal assembly at UN Government House in Jerusalem, Daniel suggests that the court was influenced by criticism of those acts in the media. The judges handed down light sentences, to show that they had not been influenced by the media. The courts also tend to leniency towards extremist political movements such as Kach, so that the movement's extreme views will not be perceived as the reason for severe sentences. This general tendency was not at work, however, when Kahane was sentenced to administrative detainment in May 1980; this sentence was a serious violation of individual rights.

In practice, the authorities' leniency tended to legitimize Kach's illegal, violent acts. When Kahane's actions expanded to include the "bunker" of Kach activists who refused to leave Yamit when the city was evacuated, as well as settlement activity in the territories, it poses a threat to the rule of law in a democratic state. Kahane is a master at utilizing the weaknesses of Israeli society for his own ends.

21

Ha'etznis Reflections from Kiryat Arba

Ha'etzni

Eliakim Ha'etzni, a nonreligious lawyer, was one of the first settlers of the Jewish city of Kiryat Arba, overlooking Hebron. A leading proponent of peaceful coexistence with the Arabs, he serves as legal counsel for many Arabs. He is a member of the Kiryat Arba Municipal Council, and supported the formation of a municipal coalition which included Kahane's Kach party after municipal elections in June 1985. Ha'etzni had been one of the leaders of *Shurat Ha'mitnadvim* (the "Volunteer Corps"), which successfully fought government corruption during the 1950's. Ha'etzni, who had been a member of the Mapai party, became, in his own words, more "extreme" after the Mapai party supported Amos Ben-Gurion, David Ben-Gurion's son, and one of the police commanders charged with corruption by *Shurat Ha'mitnadvim*. Ha'etzni was one of the first leaders of the Greater Israel movement, and is close to Gush Emunim and Gush leader Rabbi Moshe Levinger.

I met Ha'etzni in his home in Kiryat Arba. I listened to him for hours, after prodding him with provocative questions. Here is his monologue:

You ask me why Kahane was elected in the 1984, and not in

previous, elections? This is a difficult question, to which I'm not sure that I have the answer. It's cumulative. There are processes which have to mature with people, such as – making a thousand distinctions between the two – the threshold of provocation of the nonreligious, how much they will suffer the provocations of the religious, such as [driving on] the roads on the Sabbath [the subject of occasionally violent confrontations between the religious and nonreligious]. How long can a minority provoke the majority, to impose decrees, and have the majority remain silent? After crossing the threshold, this is finished.... Kahane is just a symptom. He is the antibodies which the body mobilizes against infection, which endanger and attack the body. You have to fight against infection with something strong.

What did the organized Jewish community do to the Arabs in 1948? It did things to them beyond Kahane's most terrible dreams.... Kahane's barks have no bite. The Jewish community expelled Arabs with mortars. Afterwards we killed Arabs who infiltrated at night to collect the remnants of their property, which they had abandoned at the height of the battles. We were 600,000 people. Destruction was anticipated for the Jewish community. We were in the condition of Lebanon: a war of religions. The result was a reaction. Anyone who judges the actions of the Jewish community outside of that context commits a historical crime. The stronger that Israel became, turning into a state, the more it improved in its democratic behavior, laws, and institutions. The Kfar Kassem incident [at the beginning of the Sinai campaign, in which curfew was decreed in an Arab village, and 41 curfew violators were shot] was still possible in 1956. A mini-Holocaust. There was an attempt to blot out and silence the incident: the trial [of the soldiers involved], the punishments, the early release of those who had been found guilty, the presidential pardon, the acceptance of the murderers by the public.

...There was a party press then. Today it's anarchic and unbridled. Since then in the realm of government and law, morals, and the IDF as well, Israel has progressed. The opposite of the image presented by the left. The further back you go, the worse the situation was, not as the left blurs facts, making them more beautiful. The IDF in Lebanon was the most moral army of all of Israel's wars.

The expulsion of the Arabs. Many of those "missing" [the official term applied to Arabs who left Israel in 1948] were expelled. And if they fled during the height of the war, was there any sin in that? We wiped them out and divided their property, but the Jewish lands in Hebron, which were abandoned – we found after the Six Day War that they were still registered in King Hussein's registers.

We didn't stop with the theft of lands. We also enacted laws for the expropriation of Arab lands which had been abandoned, and the High Court of Justice was quick to approve after the fact the expropriations which had been carried out in the field. In this manner we took Nazareth's land reserves, and now Nazareth's Arabs are penetrating into Upper Nazareth, because they have no choice. The Military Government served both General Security Services as tools of the party. The corruption of the Security Services, which served the party and the special clique within the clique. Israel then was a monster.

In order to understand Kahane, it is necessary to start from the beginning, from 1948, and perhaps even earlier.

The stronger Israel became, the more it entered into the yoke of the commandments, just like a boy. Israel's Bar Mitzvah was Levi Eshkol's ascension to power. He brought with him peace, compromises, a good spirit. He was good and beneficient between the right and the left. An intermission. He brought Ze'ev Jabotinsky's bones [to Israel, marking official recognition by the State of Israel for the Revisionist leader]. The state under Eshkol's regime recognized its obligations. The state had already come of age during the period of the Six Day War. The war did not corrupt, as the left claims, but rather the reverse. Since 1967, we've begun to act towards the Arabs in a more humane and responsible manner. We began to demand of ourselves a different attitude; one of law and government. It is doubtful if this was the case before 1967, especially during the time of the military government. We've reached the conclusion that there is no justification for excesses towards Arabs, as there were on the eve of the establishment of the state: different rules for the unfortunate and the oppressed. There was more law in the government after 1967. The press was freer. The attorney-generals were more independent, and even dared to call for the indictment of the prime minister. The army was more moral, and there was stronger control over it. The rule of law applied to Arabs as well, first in Israel, and then in the territories.

At some point we crossed the dividing line and swung towards the other side of the pendulum: We've deteriorated from a condition in which everything was permissible for the state to a condition in which everything is permissible against the state – from extremism to extremism. Anarchy within the realm of the law. The attorney-general. Everything is permitted. For example: Bir Zeit University. This is an open agency of the PLO, an open underground against Israel.

This permissiveness, that it is permissible to incite to the murder of Jews and civil rebellion, like those articles which are printed in the press, including the *Jerusalem Post*. It's permissible to hug and kiss Arafat during the Lebanon war, according to the opinion of the attorney-general, who doesn't give a damn.

Guilt feelings entered the vacuum. We have a guilt complex about the Arabs. We took the land from them. We've changed, in our own eyes, from those oppressed by the Arabs to oppressors. While they, the Arabs, were partners with Hitler in the Holocaust. We're Samson and they're David. We're the ones biting away. We're slowly approaching the philosophy of the PLO and Jordan: the Jews did not live in the Land of Israel, but were only passersby, wanderers. The Palestinians are the local residents, and the land belongs to them.

We are performing a self-delegitimization in our own home. Some military judges on reserve duty in Judea and Samaria are influenced by these moods. They impose ridiculous sentences on stone throwers, some of whom caused the death of Esther Ohana. Then the process of understanding which Arabs are using terror against us. Issam Sartawi. Kisses to Arafat. They're a liberation movement. Israeli journalists serve as their defenders. A war of liberation to be freed of Israel. We're depressed. We are the ones fighting against the Palestinian liberators. A split personality is even beginning to develop among IDF soldiers: as in an Israeli movie, supported by the taxpayers' money, the hero does not know whom he is supposed to shoot: an agent of the General Security Services, or a terrorist. He doesn't know who's who.

A condition of "I'm the guilty one." An entire people is attempting to place itself in the dock. Flagellation. A nation that seeks to invalidate its own motives. Seeks and finds, as well. Feels guilty. Our entire pride has suddenly become our stigma. All the concepts are changing, becoming distorted. Just as the sand became gold here, now gold is sand. Settlement, the crowning Israeli-Jewish achievement, has suddenly become the theft of Arab lands. A Jewish National Fund forest is camouflage and cover for the dispossession of Arab villagers. They're striving to fulfill a new vision: an Arab village will be built on the ruins of a kibbutz. This is how justice will be attained. Everything which was once beautiful has become ugly. Zionist Jewish myths are being shattered to foster a Palestinian myth in their stead. The late professor Jacob Talmon showed that the urge to self-destruction has been latent in the Jewish people since the sacrifice of Isaac.

The minority which thinks this way ... is aided by the press, the left, the journalists. The writing is superficial. The motifs used are the crude stereotypes which are in fashion, in the style of the People's Democracies. It's very easy to produce these en masse. Cheap, destructive fashions lead countries to destruction. Look at the Weimar republic in Germany in the 1920's, and Munich in the 1930's and 1940's. The media, the theater, literature, the cinema, and the universities, stood behind these. They impressed the entire world with the aid of superficial intellectual cliches. See the first volume of Winston Churchill's memoirs. They slaughtered Churchill. The ones who acted this way were exposed years later as Soviet agents. They were midgets in their party then. Churchill was a giant, but in those days, they were portrayed as the giants, not he. They called for "Peace in our time." They wrote editorials in the *London Times*, spoke and gave speeches in the literary clubs. Harold Lasky was one of those midgets. A Jew, an economist, political and social scientist, and an intellectual leader with great influence on the Labor party in England. Today, a generation later, it's common knowledge that they were midgets, lacking in original thought, who spoke in empty slogans. Churchill had a problem in contending with them. He found it difficult to explain his profound thought as opposed to the vocal shouters of the British "Peace Now." It's easy to formulate superficial "wisdom"; it sparkles like polished chrome. Churchill, however, had to explain matters of the spirit, which relate to the profundities of life. How can you make a popularization out of this? When Churchill spoke about the verities of life, they called this rhetoric.

This was convenient for the media: the mating of superficial, false, "wisdom" with the immediate, technical need of the media.... like the relationship now between Peace Now and the media. All of a sudden, every Arab is pitiful, and every rock thrower is a freedom fighter; they don't want to hear that the rock thrower was hired at full pay to do this work. While Israel strikes outside its borders with an iron fist, this same Israel permits the persecution of [pro-]Israeli Druze in the Golan Heights, after their annexation to Israel, just as Jews were persecuted in the Diaspora. The State is incapable of defending its citizens.

Kahane provided the answer to all these phenomena. This is the latest symptom in our society.

Once I asked Col. Zuker, a brigade commander in Judea and Samaria: If you are riding in a jeep and stones are thrown at you – the punishment according to the law which was enacted 18 years ago is life imprisonment. The rock thrower doesn't stop when you ask him. You shoot in the air, and he continues to flee. [What do you do then?] Zuker replied, I'm forbidden to shoot in the air, also.

Why do detectives in Tel Aviv, from the police's Central Unit, shoot when they suspect that a stolen vehicle is fleeing, and they hit and wound, and this is not in occupied territory? Zuker had no answer.

Every soldier serving in the reserves in Judea and Samaria carries in his pocket the orders for opening fire. They state: If rocks are thrown at you, you must break off contact. But when

170

someone burned an Arab bus in Hebron, the commander of the [army Central] Command Maj.-Gen. Uri Or came here, all trembling and shaken. The result of undermining morale, self-confidence. For example: Prof. Havah Yafah Lazarus, an expert on Islam from the Hebrew University – for her, the Cave of Mahpelah is the Ibrahimi Mosque; she doesn't know any other expression. And Judea and Samaria is the "West Bank." A syndrome. Like the operation which the Hellenizers performed to cancel circumcision, to return the foreskin. Hellenization in the direction of the Arabs and the Palestinians. The attitude that Jewish blood is cheap. People in Israel relate to all kinds of casualties, but they don't relate to those injured in road accidents. There's no one to be angry at here. This is a natural disaster, and no more. No one's guilty. A blow from Heaven. On the other hand, at the other end of the spectrum, there are those killed in the Lebanon War. Here, there are guilty ones. The murderers send them, the soldiers [who are killed]. Something happened to us. Guilt. It's connected to the syndrome of Abraham sacrificing Isaac on the altar of religion and/or homeland and/or Zionism and/or idealism. Even among the electorate of the Likud, Tehiya, and the national camp, there is a guilt feeling, specifically because they support the war in Lebanon.

Until the Kahane period, the victims of terror and the Fatah were like those killed in road accidents. Maybe we didn't feel guilt for what happened to them. Maybe we didn't do enough for the security of those within Israel. It's this way with all the victims of the PLO in Israel. They have no one to turn to, neither a person nor a place. As if they were the victims of fatal car accidents. Neither anger nor vengeance. There's no human sentiment towards anyone who does this. Why? Because the elimination of all feeling has gone this far. Their "war of liberation," and you don't know who's right. They've been shortchanged all the time. We've brought this on ourselves. We've turned into the other side's judges. Then we cease to be a side, and then they haven't done us any injustice. They only see the other side. Suicide. A bullet in the head, via intelligence and judgement.

The death of Esther Ohana by rock throwers symbolizes the beginning of the counterwave and the reaction. Therefore they remember her name as a victim of terror and the rock-throwing in Judea and Samaria. She was killed next to Jews in Judea and Samaria who don't want to forget. Others were killed by terror in regions of pre-1967 Israel, where the media blinds and blurs between good and evil.... After the death of Aaron Gross it was very difficult in the square in Hebron, near the marketplace, to drive into the heads of the defense establishment the very idea that a pillar would be erected in the center of Hebron in memory of a martyr, and that it would be written on it that he was murdered. This isn't pleasant for the Arabs, that part of the picture of the street and the scenery of Hebron would be a Jewish tombstone. In the eyes of the bleeding hearts, the tombstone is adding insult to injury. Why is a Jew in Hebron a provocation? The Arabs don't say this. They expected that we would expel them from all of Hebron. It was Sheikh Jabri, of all people, who proposed the restoration of the Abraham Avinu synagogue, which had been destroyed in the 1929 riots.... A guilt complex. We apologize all the time. Why should we provoke and irritate? This entire process is taking place among the Jews and not among the Arabs. We've gotten to such a state that even a Jewish prisoner is nothing. One prisoner for 5,000 terrorists. This is monstrous. Our self-righteous and pious claim about precious human life, and so on, facing unfathomable indifference to human life. Look at the daily record: the brutal robbery and murder of old people, shocking and rising crime, instances of hardheartedness towards the sick and the unfortunate. We're not a compassionate society. All this is so because you're not a party, only a judge, without pains and impulses, and we deserve what the terrorists did to us, because of our sins. We've gotten to such a state that a terrorist who sits in jail and is interviewed on television, and he's the nephew of Ahmed Jibril, complains that they feed him chicken every day. This is in comparison with the boy who's a POW, whom we blame for having fallen into captivity. We're also guilty for the Palestinian refugees and their existence. They're engaging in dehumanization. The artificial objectivization constitutes

172

dehumanization.

One can feel a great deal of sympathy for MK Meir Cohen-Avidov for his saying that Arab murderers should have their eyes torn out. He revealed human sentiment by his primitive statement, which was tasteless and cruel, but at least human. The left has planted within us the unfeeling robot, lacking responses and reflexes; everything is only road accidents and only we're to blame, and the same for revenge and hatred, which are human.

The government doesn't rule. The defense establishment doesn't provide defense. Israel provides its citizens with security, but not a feeling of security. We're returning to the ghetto. Our fate is not in our hands. We do not rule. We ingratiate ourselves with aliens. The Exile has crept into us, and acts from within.

Kahane's voters are divided into two: a small part consists of hooligans, who need action and the fist, which symbolizes their desires. The white trash in the world always attacks someone inferior to it. Kahane also found for himself a national title. In this manner he disperses the feelings of shame. He grew from a small nucleus to a seat in the Knesset. There's another segment of his voters: fundamentalists. Bodies such as Mercaz Harav [a yeshivah which is a Gush Emunim stronghold], Tehiya, the Likud, Morasha, or Gush Emunim are too watery for them, watered-down Biblical wine. Kahane's voters really believe that democracy and the Torah, and the Israeli Declaration of Independence and the Torah, are contradictory. They accept things at face value. They want to institute the rule of the Torah in the same manner as did Joshua ben Nun: "You shall not let a soul remain alive" [Deut. 20:16].

Kahane would not have made it to the Knesset if he had remained with only these two categories of voters. The third element, which fed on everything which I have already mentioned, is what brought him to the Knesset: the average voter in the street, who, for all manner of reasons, has a clear-eyed view of the situation. He sees Kahane as the red flag before the bull in the arena. He believes that Kahane will correct all the faults. A serious act has to occur in front of the government so that it will awaken to action, the worst taboo has to be used. Kahane is this taboo. "See, you've been warned: we brought Kahane to the Knesset." All this is so there will be a balance to the negative phenomena, the flagellation, Yossi Sarid and Co. Perhaps there will have to be ten like him in the Knesset in order to attain a balance. The person voting for Kahane says, the greater the commotion, the surer I am that I was right in voting the way I did. I wanted to startle the government, so that it will return to rule, return to Zionism, cease to be Palestinian. The reflex worked. And if this isn't enough, and it doesn't help, we'll put another few like Kahane in the Knesset.

You ask me what I've got against Kahane? Here's my answer: his attitude towards the Arabs. I want to live with them. A state clean of Arabs is a Nazi state. I'm aghast by what's written in the Bible about the expulsion of foreigners. Do I have to do everything that's written in the Bible? I don't need those interpreting Joshua ben Nun. I'm not religiously observant. The religious will tell you that Kahane's statements are horrible. They're more authentic than I am. Don't wave in my face the claim that this is written in the Bible.... I understand Judaism differently. Not trampling over everything like this. Zionism has a moral and humane basis, and so does Judaism. I would not have been a Zionist if they had told me that Zionism also means genocide, expelling a people from its land. The end does not justify the means. The question is, which end and what means. Auschwitz for the Arabs? If this were so, I would quickly return to the Diaspora. I'm not willing to pay such a price for a state. Such a means does not justify the end. There is no such sanctified end in Judaism.

We have a moral problem with the Arabs; to say the reverse would be a lie. But the cliches of the left move in the opposite direction. The Palestinians have the bad luck to live in one land with the only people who have survived from antiquity, with power and ability, who found no other place to live, and who landed here. We have a moral problem, that we found the Arabs here. A planned-out, mathematical, German solution by a cruel Zionism is impossible. What the left does is against itself. It wants to throw the Jews out from here, and the people swing

174

between the two poles: Kahane's cruelty towards the Arabs, and the left's cruelty towards the Jews – and I'm in the middle.

We have to say to the Arabs: Whoever wants to make peace, may make peace. Joshua ben Nun was interpreted as follows: he offered the enemies peace, and when they did not want this, he ordered their destruction. I don't want to return to the period of the monstrous Joshua ben Nun. This is what Kahane does. He severs himself from the reality of the 20th century. This is monstrous, it is reminiscent of the techniques of the Nazis: to take images from Joshua ben Nun and to shift them here, to our time.

Kahane is a caricature. He can make people compare themselves to Joshua ben Nun and turn into murderers.

The Arabs must be treated as people just like us, within the context of law, order, and government. I can't understand Kahane's saying that the Arab is not a human being. He proposes a law against mixed marriages and warns the public against racial defilement. There isn't any racial philosophy here. The Arabs and we are descended from the same race. It's non-sense to talk of this. His blood contains much non-Semitic blood, and this is the case with the Arabs as well. The Arab problem is political. Here is where the danger lies: relating to the political conflict as if it were a religious conflict, or a conflict between people who were born with additional rights owed them by their Jewishness. This arouses [anger], and I can't accept such a thesis for Judaism, for Zionism, for humanity. This can lead to bloodshed, which I oppose. We don't have the concepts of Lebanon and murders. Murders among the Arabs of the territories have decreased greatly, since they've learned from our way of life....

Let the government enforce the law, and plant security and a feeling of security among Israelis; it must not reveal weakness or desperation. The problem between us and the Arabs must be resolved in a practical manner, using modern, rational, thought. We must not confuse the solution with religious and emotional subjects, which cannot be expressed logically. There are many answers to the political problem, on condition that the Land of Israel belongs to the Jewish people. This is axiomatic, and we must begin from this. If the Arab says that this is Palestine, that it belongs to the Palestinians, and that there will be war – then there will be war. Each war deepened our hold on the land of Israel. If they could, the Arabs would have *ex post facto* prevented each war which they conducted against us. They paid a heavy price. We have no reason to be frustrated by the wars. The 500,000 Jews living in Germany during World War I lost 12,000 during that war – more than in all of Israel's wars. In order to establish and maintain the State of Israel, we paid with fewer dead than those Jews who fell in foreign armies, in wars which were not theirs. A Jew fires on a Jew in the armies of the rest of the world – for what, and for whom? The Arabs lost, while we gained, from each war. There is one restriction in the political battle between us: the Land of Israel for the Jewish people. Arabs who do not want to live with us, and who reveal hostility towards us in their actions, must be removed from here. This is the antithesis of Kahane's philosophy. He wants to remove the Arabs, not for their acts, but solely because they are Arabs, aliens...

What is to be done with the Arabs?

There are things which we cannot weigh on the scales of utility. Even if I did not have an answer I would not expel them. There are things which you cannot do. There are prohibitions which are binding on society just as they are binding on the individual. The Arabs of Judea and Samaria cannot be granted the right to vote. Israeli Arabs have already been granted this, and it cannot be revoked. If there is a contradiction here, why, life is full of contradictions. I waived two-thirds of Israel to the Arabs. Jordan is their state. There is where the Palestinian state will be. The Arabs living in Israel will have Palestinian passports, but – as at the present – they will vote there, in Amman. Half of the Jordanian parliament has been Palestinian for a long time. The kingdom is only called "Jordan." We should recall the United Nations recommendation from 1947: the Arabs who live in the State of Israel will vote in the Arab state, and the opposite. This would be accompanied by an economic union between the two states in the western Land of Israel. Today the Jewish population equals the Arab population, including Jordan. The UN recommendations must be carried out, along with moving the border to the Jordan River. A Jew who wants to live in Jordan will vote for the Knesset.

And if the Arabs refuse such a solution?

Tell me, have they already accepted Jaffa as belonging to Israel and the Jews?

I am not worried by their number, and I am not nervous because they won't vote for the Knesset. Let them know this.

Kahane and the left play with demography. They share an impure alliance of hatred of Arabs. One feeds off the other. The Arabs have not grown in the western part of the Land of Israel since 1967. They have remained one-third of the entire population in Israel and the territories. The rise in their standard of living will drown them in luxury. A woman who has graduated high school will not give birth to a dozen. The more that the two societies draw closer to each other, economic development will become greater, and the Arab birth rate will decrease. This is happening before our very eyes. Before the inevitable expulsion of the Arab, in Kahane's language, has the Jew in Israel already done everything to increase his own birth rate? If we were to invest a tiny bit of our talents in subjects such as defense, the reserves, settlement, and the IDF (all of these are part of our very lives, since we couldn't exist without them), we would reach good solutions. We haven't done this because of a weakening of the will, because of the brainwashing by the left. The prohibition on abortions is not progress. Hundreds of thousands of children have been lost in this manner; the same is true for immigration to, and the prevention of emigration from, Israel. Before we become a monster which uproots residents from their land and expels them, there are other alternatives. And what have you proposed? Moving them beyond the border, where they'll be PLO.

Kahane's method is to use disgusting slogans, just like the left. Slogans like these take hold, since they are simple, and easily understandable. The average Arab wants to live with us in peace. I know this from my living in Kiryat Arba. But both the doves and the hawks attach a PLO image to him, which he doesn't deserve. In order to get rid of the Arabs from Judea and

Samaria, the Jewish dove in Israel attaches a PLO image to the Arab, just as Kahane does in order to get rid of him. This is not the truth. This is not just. It doesn't correspond to reality. There are a few who haven't reconciled themselves to us. Citizenship should be cancelled for the latter. And when a few dozen will be gotten rid of, over the border, there will be quiet, and Kahane will have no excuse to claim the Arabs are a danger. The average Arab fears expulsion from the Zionist hell to the Arab paradise more than anything. The General Security Services has a list of a few dozen inciters who pay children to throw rocks. In this manner, they work for Kahane.

I was greatly encouraged by the 1984 election results. Despite everything, people voted for the Likud. This was a purely ideological vote, of which the Kahanistic reaction was a part. We are a healthy people. A vote which is not willing to reconcile itself to, or accept, self-destruction. The skeptics, who gave up on the Likud, turned to Kahane and the Tehiya. The Alignment said that it wanted to return territories to Jordan, and many therefore did not vote for it, despite the fact that it had built more in Judea, Samaria, and Sinai than had the Likud. Those who had high hopes for the Likud and were disappointed from the way it conducted itself when in power went to Kahane. The Likud government until 1984 can be characterized as a right wing government with two left hands. Only Ariel Sharon built in Judea and Samaria, since he didn't grow up among the Revisionists, who belittled themselves before the left when they attained power. He was born in Kfar Malal, a bastion of the left. The Likud is suitable for living rooms but not for ruling.

Kahane's strength is in the reaction. The body's providing a reaction in the 1984 elections was a sign that it is healthy. Woe to us if the voter had not reacted to all the poisons in the left. Kahane is a counter-poison, and they vote for him as such.

My forecast: Kahane will become even more powerful. He will be stopped only when the government assumes its responsibilities.

22

Kahane: The Man and his Motives

Dr. Ehud Sprinzak, a senior lecturer in political science at Hebrew University, has researched and written extensively on extremist movements, including Kach. He describes Kahane as "a bundle of opposing elements." As a rabbi, he provides spiritual authority and an air of legitimacy to underground activities. Inspired by him, Kahane's people employ violence and terror against Arabs in Israel and its territories. Extremism, for Kahane, evokes the attention and media coverage he finds essential.

On June 25, 1969, one year after Kahane founded the Jewish Defense League, the *New York Times* called the JDL an "American nightmare," and its leader, a "political demagogue." Jewish leaders in the United States referred to the JDL as the "Jewish Ku Klux Klan," and its members, as "unadorned fascists."

Excelling neither in administration nor supervision, Kahane prefers gimmicks and flashy acts to sustained projects. He is wary of associates who show qualities of leadership and the potential to challenge his position in JDL's hierarchy. Those who question his one-man rule are anathema to Kahane. In both Israel and the United States, he changes leaders with dizzying rapidity. Kahane and his former associates mince no words in their open hostility to each other.

Fred Horowitz, whose loan to Kahane was never repaid, warns that at least half of what Kahane says, both in person and in print, must be discounted. Kahane once confided to him that he addresses himself to the lowest common denominator of any population because it's easiest to get support at that level. According to Horowitz, Kahane's primary motive is revenge. All his life he has sought the recognition from the Jewish community that his father did not attain. He wants the Jewish community to pay for his father's disgrace. How? Through donations for Kahane's personal use, disguised as contributions for JDL activities.

Dov Sperling, an activist on behalf of Soviet Jews who himself immigrated to Israel from the USSR in December 1968, was mobilized by Kahane in autumn of 1970, for a series of lectures at American campuses and synagogues. Sperling spent three weeks with Kahane, part of that time in Kahane's home. "Even then," Sperling recalls, "I didn't like Kahane. His behavior towards his members and supporters was terrible. He belittled them. When one of his activists was arrested, he didn't bother defending him, nor did he go to the trouble of finding a lawyer for him. Once I learned who Kahane was, I left him.

"When we met him at the beginning of 1970," Sperling adds, "Kahane didn't talk at all about the struggle to open the gates of the USSR for the immigration of Jews to Israel, although both Geula Cohen and I stressed the issue with him. He appeared unmoved, viewing the issue as a publicity stunt."

Indeed, Kahane's acts are often improvisations of the moment, subject to transient events and his own alternating moods and whims. For the sake of headlines, he switched from protecting New York neighborhoods from anti-Semites to terrorist acts against the PLO, moving easily from the PLO to anti-Soviet activity. Shortly after the JDL was founded to defend local Jewish neighborhoods, the organization broke through its geographical boundaries to "go international." Kahane's new philosophy: the JDL was now responsible for the well-being of Jews everywhere. When reports streamed in about the Zionist renaissance in the USSR, Kahane joined the struggle, managing to keep his name in the headlines. Once his earlier targets were exhausted for publicity purposes or showed signs of retaliation, Kahane abandoned them for new causes. The Russians were an easy target at the time. Their installations and personnel in New York were inadequately defended. More importantly, Kahane preferred rooftop sniping into the apartments of Soviet diplomats over the tediousness of patrolling Jewish neighborhoods.

Quick results are what Kahane wants, consumed by his hunger for attention from the media. Celebrating his election to the Knesset in 1984, Kahane held a press conference during which he waved a Bible and pointing to it, brazenly declared: "Whoever goes against Kahane acts against this!" He then stopped abruptly at the height of his diatribe to strike a better pose for a cameraman.

Asked once by a journalist if he didn't fear that his people would become victims of the violence he champions, Kahane replied that goals could not be won without victims. "When there is a need for violence," he declared, "people are willing to fight and make sacrifices." Yet senior police officers at Israeli National Headquarters who are familiar with Kahane, sum the man up in one word: "Coward."

Shmuel Katz, a member of the Irgun Tzva'i Leumi command, a Herut member of the first Knesset, and information advisor to former Prime Minister Begin, says he's "convinced that Kahane is insane. There is a small chance of his growing in power, but if election laws are changed, he'll be cut off. Everyone knows about Kahane's obsession for publicizing himself and about his links with the FBI."

The most accurate analysis of Kahane, surprisingly enough, comes from the Kach leader himself. In 1973, he told Shlomo Russ (Raziel), author of a comprehensive study on Kahane: "I'm a spectacular failure in every sense. Nothing that we wanted to do went over because the American Jewish leaders didn't have the brains, the vision, the courage. We said the right things. We said the truth and we had the vision, but we couldn't pull it off: not in poverty, not in education, not in anything. It is not enough to say that we moved the establishment to start (adopting issues like Soviet Jewry). It's too little, too late."

Russ concludes this section of his study with the remark: "Perhaps later generations will be kinder in judging Kahane."

American media are less charitable; they compare Kahane's speeches to Borscht belt routines by Jewish stand-up comics.

Kahane tells American journalists that he is rational, but is glad to have the image of a madman. When the JDL was founded, Kahane asserts, he and his followers were happy to be labelled a "tough gang" or "terrorists." In a speech on September 9, 1984 at the Silver Springs Jewish Center in Washington, Kahane asked: "How, how do we get the Arabs out?

"Picture Arabs turning on the radio one morning to hear that the new Minister of Defense is Meir Kahane. How will we get them out? When they hear that, they'll pack themselves. I understand the Arabs. They understand me... We both can't understand Jews... They say, 'He's crazy.' I like that image. I don't want a nice image. The Arabs understand what Kach is!..."

Kahane elaborated on the same theme at his trial before the military court in Ramallah [reported in the *Jewish Press*, August 29, 1980]. Calling his trial "a humiliation for all who take part in it," Kahane continued: "The Arabs wait for the Jews to imprison me for they understand me. For they fear me. They fear my reaching the Knesset and then the government. They hope you will stop me. They understand me and I understand them. But neither of us can understand this government...

"I understand the Arab. He sincerely believes that we – you and I – are thieves. Those who preach coexistence, he the donkey and me riding him, hold him in contempt. You do not buy the Arab's love with economic progress... He is not an animal; he is a human being... He will become a majority in the land and the Knesset because this is a democracy, thanks to us... He must leave or we will..."

According to Shlomo Russ, only Kahane's closest family knows the reason for his blind hatred of Arabs, a reason he guards as secret. Members of Kahane's family were murdered by Arabs during the bloody disturbances of 1938 in Mandatory Palestine.

182

In 1938, members of a well-known branch of the Kahane family in Safed attended the wedding of a daughter of the Kahane family in Tel-Aviv. On the way back to Safed, near the Arab village of Majd-el-Krum, armed Arabs stopped the taxi carrying Meir Kahane's cousins – a mother, daughter, and granddaughter – and murdered them in cold blood. Only a two-and-a-half year old girl survived (Rivka Yaniv, who currently lives in Israel). Her mother, Tziporah Kahane, and her grandmother were murdered, together with a 14-year-old cousin. Tziporah was Meir Kahane's aunt, the wife of Mordecai Kahane, his father Yehezkiel's brother. Mordecai later immigrated to the United States where he lived for years in Yehezkiel's home, before returning to Israel after the establishment of the state. Kahane never speaks of this, for fear of being charged with prejudice against Arabs. He prefers to maintain that his ideology springs from a purely rational analysis of the Israeli situation.

In the United States, Kahane's speaking style is flooded with pathos. He asks questions such as: "Do you know the fear and terror caused by the mixed marriages and social life which exist in Israel? Do you know the terror of prostitution, where all the prostitutes are Jewish, while the pimps are Arabs?" Tears fill his listeners' eyes when he tells of meeting an elderly Moroccan Jew in Israel, who told him his two daughters had married Arabs, and that he had never believed such a thing could happen in the Holy Land. Now that his audience is listening, scarcely breathing, Kahane confides that Arabs in Israel kidnap Jewish women. He tells them he has "good reason to believe" that a girl named Ayala Alfasi is being held by Arabs in the Gaza Strip where she is forced into prostitution. He blames "spineless" Israeli authorities for doing nothing, and concludes by wondering how many other Jewish girls are being held in Gaza.

In Israel, Kahane and his followers use the issue of sexual relations with Arabs as a weapon to silence opposition. When Israel radio reporter Carmela Menashe posed questions that provoked Kahane at a press conference, he refrained from answering, but had his bodyguards shout: "You sleep with Arabs!"

In Brooklyn, Kahane presents himself as the Biblical hero Samson, smiting the anti-Semites. In Israel, he strikes the pose of the prophet Jeremiah, lashing the Israelis for their "perverted ways" and their "sins."

In 1971, Kahane proclaimed to an Israeli journalist in New York: "An Israeli who identifies with Arabs and thinks that the liberated territories were stolen from them, has no right to live in Israel. He is an Exile Jew. It is impossible to differentiate between the state and the Torah because the State of Israel was not established by force of the United Nations resolutions, but by force of the Torah and Divine will."

In October 1972, an interviewer for *Playboy Magazine* asked Kahane about the charge by some Jewish leaders that his readiness to resort to violence contradicts the principles of Judaism.

"When some so-called leader gets up and emotes about what is and is not Jewish, it pains me," Kahane replied, "because I can't stand ingorance. If he owned an insurance business, I wouldn't have the chutzpah to argue with him about insurance. So let him not tell me, a rabbi, what is Jewish. Gandhi, a pacifist, was not a Jew. Moses was a Jew and he smote the Egyptians." Asked how far he would be willing to go in the use of violence, Kahane responded: "As far as necessary. If an American Nazi Party leader posed a clear and present danger to American Jews, not to assassinate such a person would be one of the most immoral courses I could imagine."

How could he take upon himself the responsibility of deciding whether or not to take another's life, Kahane was asked.

"You have an obligation to do things in a nice way," he replied. "You have to give your antagonist an opportunity to change. Once you've given him that chance and it doesn't work, you have an obligation – not just a right, but an **obligation** – to move on to something that is not nice."

Kahane agreed with the interviewer that such reasoning could, indeed, be used to justify whatever one thinks is right.

"Then the only difference between you and, say, the American Nazi Party is that they're wrong and you're right?" the interviewer asked.

"I can't put it any better than that," replied Kahane.

184

23

Summing up

In the realms of fiction, the hero with the "fatal flaw" is a staple. While Meir Kahane has great powers of persuasion – power which could have been utilized productively for the good of his people – he suffers not from one, but from numerous major flaws, which have made him the man he is, a distinct menace to Judaism and to Israeli society.

He is a user of others. The list of those he has discarded after getting as much as he could out of them is a long one – and keeps growing longer, as he replaces one "trusted" compatriot by another. In a seemingly never-ending procession, we find Zweibon and Dolinsky, co-founders with Kahane of the JDL; Murry Wilson, one of his main financial backers; those charged with the Iris Kones murder who were not even provided with legal aid; Amihai Paglin and the failed arms smuggling plan; Yossi Dayan; Yossi Schneider; Yoel Lerner…

If, indeed, Kahane has goals, the means to achieve those goals never seem to have bothered him. If cementing an alliance with one of the heads of the Mafia, Joe Colombo, served to pay Kahane's bail, he had no hesitation to accept the money tendered – and who knows where that money came from! Should the innocent be harmed or even killed, it is purely incidental and of no consequence. Kahane has still not expressed remorse over the death of Iris Kones. He gave three of his hooligans $500 to pay the rent for a car used in shooting at an Arab bus – and never even bothered to find out what "brave exploit" they had been up to!

What **does** bother him? Not being in the news. He quotes the old American maxim, "I don't care what you say about me, as long as you spell my name correctly." He jumps from one bandwagon to another, reaping whatever publicity he can in the process. He has supported neighborhood patrols, protests for Soviet Jewry, and – in Israel – an "Arab-**rein**"* country. All these have been "hot" issues, ones that have guaranteed him the media coverage that he craves. When papers didn't offer enough coverage of Meir Kahane, he himself – writing under pseudonyms – published laudatory articles in the Jewish Press – about himself!

Yet the man who preaches that there is but one righteous person (none other than Meir Kahane) and that everyone else is evil or in error, has – at the least – feet of clay. While Kahane has few compunctions about others serving prison sentences for actions taken with his active or passive connivance, he has a pathological fear of serving time himself.

He preaches the imposition of Torah laws on Israel – and disregards those laws constantly in his personal life. He seems to have no compunctions in treating others' money as his own; in borrowing and not repaying loans; in raising funds for a yeshiva and then diverting them to his election campaigns; in taking JDL funds, and – without approval using them to pay his legal expenses.

He rails incessantly against Arabs and their "lust" for Jewesses, of Arabs pimping for Jewish prostitutes, in identical tones to those used by the Nazis against the Jews and the southern whites against the blacks. Yet he was not above "cruising" the streets of New York as Michael King and having a love affair with Gloria/Estelle D'Argenio. And this same representative of Jewish honor and pride willingly hid his very Jewishness in order to better find willing non-Jewish females.

He has written that one of the "four cornerstones of [Jewish]

* free.

186

Redemption," is "the resolute decision to love each and every Jew as [one]self." Yet, having evidently decided that he has run out of non-Jewish demons, he has now extended his nets even further afield – to the extent of openly preaching the murder of those Jews whose views he despises.

This is Meir Kahane.

24

Kahane in his Own Words

Meir Kahane's book *Forty Years* is full of inciting and racist statements, Messianic writing with hastily-delivered judgements and apocalyptic predictions. The number 40, either years or days, is mentioned many times in the Bible: the forty days of Nineveh, the 40 years of Israel's wandering in the wilderness, the 40 days at Mount Sinai. When Kahane was in Ramle Prison under administrative detention, he devoted much thought to these 40 years. The Divine spirit suddenly came to him, and the false prophet began to speak. He talks of a 40-year "period of grace," and calls upon the Jew to set his house in order: "That state of Israel which rose up in the year 1948, I am convinced, is the beginning, not only of the redemption, but of the grace period granted us ... a last opportunity to reverse needless disaster, to bring the redemption with grandeur and majesty.... And time ticks away and the decision is in our hands."

The "Hellenists" (Kahane's enemies) have created in the Holy land a "hideous, Hebrew caricature of foreign, gentilized, culture." Kahane writes of the Jew in the Exile who "prefers the impurity and contamination of the lands of the nations" to the separate Jewish destiny and homeland. "He sits in his newly chosen land, wallowing in the flesh of the gentile pots, even as his Maker prepares to sweep them away in a flood of fire. He sits in the bosom of the gentile [world], emulating all its falsehood, embracing its paganism and idolatries as passionately as the foreign woman he takes for a mate."

Perhaps when Kahane wrote this passage he was thinking of himself, and his passion for the young, beautiful – and "foreign" – model whom he desired, Estelle Donna Evans, who committed suicide when Kahane broke off relations with her.

FORTY YEARS

(selected passages)
Forty. Again and again, the number forty connected to sin and punishment... "as was done to Adam who sinned, was deserving of death and was punished with forty. For the world was cursed due to his sin, forty curses: ten for Adam, ten for Eve, ten for the serpent and ten for the land" ... And so convinced I am that, just as twice in the past He gave us a period of grace, so too, today, we have been granted it. And it becomes clearer and clearer to me that, once again, it is forty years; forty years of warning, admonition, opportunity. The final chance....

And so, a Jewish state rose from the crematoria and ashes, not because we deserved it, but because the gentile did. Because the punishment and awesome wrath of G-d were being prepared for a world that had mocked and humiliated the name of the L-rd, G-d of Israel.

That state of Israel which rose up in the year 1948, I am convinced, is the beginning, not only of the redemption, but of the grace period granted us. In the very marrow of my bones I feel that the Al-mighty, in His infinite mercy and goodness, gives us the final, beseeching opportunity to turn needless suffering into glorious and instant redemption. Not for nothing did Rabbi Eliezer say (Sanhedrin 99a): "The days of the Messiah are **forty years**, as it is said: 'Forty years did I quarrel with a generation...'" ...

The true finality, the magnificent era of the Messiah, comes to fruition gloriously and majestically and breathtakingly only if we cleave to the great axiom: "If you walk in my statutes... I will give peace in the land." (Leviticus 26)... "But if you will not hearken unto Me ... I will appoint terror over you." (ibid.) This is the choice; the only choice. All the rest is nonsense. And time ticks away and the decision is in our hands....

If it is true that the forty years began with the rise of the State – how many years are left? ...

A world war becomes inevitable and its price is measured in billions of lives. The World-Exile stands on the precipice, moving immutably towards a war of fire that will exterminate nations and decimate lands. **And all of this must be.**

It is inevitable. All of history – that which was, is and will be – the Al-mighty decrees. And the aweful catastrophe, as Divine punishment and vengeance, must be....

And the Jew? He sits in the volcano that is the Exile, even as from within its bowels the rumblings begin and the lava laps his feet. The Jew sits. He understands nothing. The Al-mighty prepares the cup for the gentile and the Jew, brilliantly impervious to sense, insists on supping from it. So be it. So shall it be....

Who listens? In Iran, a wealthy Jewish community pays the price for refusing to flee the profane fleshpots of the Persian exile, preferring their rugs to the Israeli carpet of Jewish soil. And in South Africa, Jews who luxuriate in the comforts of apartheid refuse to think of the sinking of Rhodesia into the sea of Zimbabwe, and close their minds to the bloodbath that is building in the minds of some 20 million Blacks. The bell tolls for them, too....

An American empire that luxuriated for three decades in material comforts unparallelled in history – declines, totters.... There is a deep malaise in the Golden land.... And within segments of the American society, the reaction begins.... Who is to blame for the descent of the once-absolute world power into a position of military and strategic inferiority? ... It will not be difficult to find a scapegoat who has been linked to liberalism, disarmament, moderation in international affairs. He is called The Jew....

The Jews against the Hellenists. The real struggle.

The dream of materialism fills the streets and the acrid smell of yearning for pleasure assails the nostrils. In the parlor, on the bus, in the cafe, the talk is of money and what it can buy. The gentile world of magical sensualism and gratification of desires fills the bowels with a painful need and the holiness of Israel is exchanged for the dream of pagan America.... and the purity of the Chosen People is exchanged for the material vomit of Los Angeles....

The kibbutz produced a Hebrew-speaking Hellenist who trampled Sinai in the dust even as he worshipped at the Pantheon of the *goy*.... *HIS* child sees not the slightest difference between Jew and non-Jew, not the slightest reason not to marry the Swedish or German gentile volunteer who works on the kibbutz.... If the Educator of the Army of Israel [the reference is to former IDF Chief Education Officer Mordechai Bar-On – trans.] sees nothing wrong in the Arab intellectual and anti-Zionist his daughter married, what shall his students say?... Children of Zion who suddenly find Jesus in Tel Aviv and pagan Indian idols in Jerusalem...

Israelis. What surprise that they march for a "peace" that is insanity and call for concessions to our enemies?... A people that has cut itself from its past has no future....

And the reality is an alarming growth in emigration figures, **yerida**...

For the cows of Dizengoff there can never be enough of the silks and dresses and gold and silver and good life of the gentile west, of the nakedness of gentile culture, of the throwing off of holiness and modesty....

Peace Now! Peace Yesterday! Peace in Six Hours! Peace, please, O gentile...! Do you not see how much we love you; why do you not love us? Peace Now, because there is no G-d. Peace Now, because we need the *goy*....

... the Jewish people prostrates itself before the feet of the gentile. All in the belief that we raise our eyes unto Washington, that from the American comes forth our salvation [cf. Psalms 121:1 – trans.]. All because we believe that the survival of Israel rests in the hands of the gentiles in the United States....

American largess will shrink in the wake of the economic disintegration, which no Administration can stem.... The reality is that America will – not necessarily through hatred or anti-Semitism – become the major enemy of Israel. And there is nothing, no amount of concessions, that will change this....

Fear begets fear; retreat guarantees retreat; pressure brings forth pressure....

There is no "Palestine" or people of that name. We feared to say it. We will pay dearly....

The Arab becomes the immutable reality that makes strong Zionists run and weep in their closets. He is the ghost of the basic contradiction between a Jewish-Zionist state and western democracy. He is the nightmare for the Hellenist who shrieks that in a democracy the Arab has a right to become a majority and to peacefully undo the Jewish State that the Declaration of Independence of Israel creates...

Pitiful Jews of no faith! Sad and tortured Hellenists! You wish to see reality? Get thee to the Galilee and to the Little Triangle, where **today**, sit a majority of Arabs, dreaming, yearning for the day when they are the masters of the state. Go to the cities of Acre, Ramle, Lydda, Upper Nazareth, Jaffa. And Jerusalem. See the deniers of Israel quietly and rapidly grow....

They will make use of them [the democratic rights of the Arabs] to eliminate Israel though peace, and in the meantime, the Galilee and Little Triangle of Israel will become hotbeds of irredentism and national demands for self-determination, marked by riots, attacks and dead Jews and Arabs....

And daily the Ishmaelite adds to Hillul Hashem [the desecration of the Name of God] that is expressed in the profanity of his roaming of land, seeking out Jewish women to bed and, sometimes, to wed them. The Jewish women who live as wives of the Ishmaelites in Arab villages are joined by the countless others ... who serve the Ishmaelite's sexual pleasures without benefit of bridal canopy....

These are the realities of a state that lost its way. But who speaks of these things and who tells them to the blissfully ignorant tourists who come to touch the Wall and gape at Masada? And who speaks of it to the Jewish children? And who is prepared to see the bitter and painful truth?...

A leader who is capable of speaking or writing on the problems of the Jew without mention of G-d, is at best an ignoramus or a fool. Turn from him; flee from him! He guarantees only national tragedy and disaster. Reject him!...

The fate of the Jew rests always and only upon the question of his faithfulness to G-d and His commandments, and until the end of time, that will always be the key to tragedy or redemption....

There is a G-d in the universe. This is the most fundamental and relevant fact for the Jew. Upon this and only upon this can he build his personal and national life and hope....

Fear of the gentile. Fear of angering the nations. This is the Law that comes out of the Exile. This is the teaching that impedes the entering of the Messiah – today....

The adoption of foreign, gentilized concepts by a Jewish state invites the vomiting out of a people, opens the doors to a national tragedy....

Jewishness, not neo-Hellenism. Holiness, not the vomit of gentilization....

The Jewish people sits together in a vessel. He who knocks a hole in the hull through desecration of G-d's law sends us all into the waves.

THEY MUST GO

(selected passages)
August 1, 1980. Ramle Prison.

...The spectacular drop in the Jewish birthrate since 1948 has been almost solely due to the negative Ashkenazic influence on the Sephardic women....

In 1976 the U.S. Library of Congress, in a study of the Arab-Jewish population, predicted that even if Israel were to give up all the liberated lands, the Arabs within the State of Israel would become a majority in 100 years. *That was based on an annual net immigration of 25,000.* Israel is nowhere near such a thing, and with economic chaos already in the land, great efforts will be needed to keep the number of emigrants from exceeding the number of new arrivals. Seventy years is a much more practical figure for that Arab majority. Why should the Arab grow more moderate?...

And it was as the *Jewish* state that Israel came into being. The very assumption of a *Jewish* state guaranteed that it cannot permit the Arab minority to become a majority....

The longtime Israeli expert on Arab affairs Tzvi El-Peleg wrote, after the Land Day Rebellion: "They [the Arabs] knew how to conceal the enmity and at the proper time to allow it to burst forth. As long as the time had not yet arrived for the enmity to come into the open, everything went peacefully. Correct relations, elaborate hospitality...." ...

And so in January 1979 Meir Har-Zion, one of the best-known heroes of the Israeli army, wrote concerning the Arabs: "I do not say we should put them on trucks or kill them.... We must create a situation in which for them, it is not worth living here, but rather in Jordan or Saudi [sic] or any other Arab state."

Har-Zion was applauded by Israeli's [sic] most famous songwriter, Naomi Shemer ("Jerusalem of Gold"), in an article in the Labor newspaper *Davar* (February 9, 1979): "Arab emigration from Israel, if done with mutual respect and positive agreement ... can be the correct answer."

And during a debate in the Knesset on Arab terrorism in the territories, Likud Knesset member Amnon Linn said (May 18, 1976): "We should begin mass expulsion of entire communities that participated in demonstrations and riots – and transfer them across the border. This is said for women, men, and children."

They are still a minority of public voices and have not yet understood the totality of what must be done...

·... the election of a strong, iron-handed government whose reputation and determination to implement this program at all cost are known to the Arab will keep resistance to a minimum....

The State of Israel is not a "political" creation. *It is a religious one.* The Arabs of Israel represent *Hillul Hashem* in its starkest form....

Tragedy will be ours *if we do not* move the Arabs out. The great redemption can come immediately and magnificently if we do that which G-d demands. One of the great yardsticks of *real*

194

Jewish faith in this time of momentous decision is our willingness to reject fear of man in favor of awe of G-d and remove the Arabs from Israel....

And then David removed Goliath's head from his shoulders and removed humiliation from Israel. Let us remove the Arabs from Israel and bring the redemption....

STATEMENT OF PRINCIPLES OF THE KACH MOVEMENT

The Chosen People
The Jewish People, special, chosen, holy, and supreme – to return to our children the Jewish pride and the self-respect which were the portion of the Jews of the Oriental communities and of Eastern Europe, before they were stolen from them by the governments of Israel; the destruction of spiritual poverty, by the return to the G-d of Israel, to faith, to the Torah, and to the commandments; the return to the splendor and magnificence inherent in the awareness that the Jewish People is the Chosen People; true Jewish education for all, so that every child in every neighborhood will arise and declare: "How good to be a good Jew! How happy are we, how good is our lot!"

Arabs to Arabia – Jews to Zion
The transfer of the Arabs from all parts of Eretz Israel. The Arabs' presence in Israel ensures hatred, disturbances, and bloodshed. It is a time bomb, threatening the existence of the Zionist enterprise. The Arabs living in Eretz Israel must therefore be transferred to the Arab countries. The danger of their becoming a majority in the State as a result of their natural increase is already a real danger now. The transformation of Israel to "Palestine" in a "democratic" manner must be prevented. Coexistence between Jews and Arabs is possible only by means of separation: Arabs to Arabia and Jews to Zion!! Until then, the obligation of alternate service to the IDF for a three-year period must be imposed on them, and the granting of National Insurance only to Jews, by its transferral to the Jewish Agency.

The transfer of the Arabs from Israel will bring us closer to our third goal.

195

The Elimination of the Disgrace of Poverty
We cannot accept a situation in which tens of thousands of Jews find themselves in poverty and distress, with their children going down the path of crime, violence, and prostitution, at the same time that others are drowning in a sea of luxury. The neighborhoods must be organized into a powerful force which shall participate in political decisions; the monetary benefits granted to Arabs must be cancelled, and the billions which are given to the Arab sector must be channeled to Jews in distress, in order to solve the problems of young couples, the elderly, marginal youth, educational frameworks, the rehabilitation of prisoners, etc.

Sovereignty and Mastery
The imposition of Israeli sovereignty over all the liberated parts of Israel, i.e., the immediate annexation of Judea and Samaria, the Gaza District, Sinai, and the Golan Heights. Making a reality of the right of every Jew to settle anywhere in Eretz Israel. Not one step of retreat.

Cancellation of the Surrender Agreements
The complete invalidation of the Camp David agreements; non-recognition of them or of any autonomy plan in the context of which the Arabs will be offered any form of independence within Eretz Israel. The basing of any negotiations with the Arabs on their recognition of the mastery of the Jewish People over all of Eretz Israel. A fierce struggle against the continuation of the retreat, and the demand to return to the lines which preceded the agreements, in order to return the oil wells in the Sinai region to the people.

Terror Against Terror
An antiterror organization will be founded, with the goal of repaying them sevenfold for all their sins.

The Temple Mount
The removal of all foreigners from the Temple Mount. The cancellation of the disgraceful situation in which the Arabs have

196

de facto established a Palestinian state in the heart of Jerusalem, on the site most holy to the Jewish People: the Temple Mount. The preparation of the infrastructure – material and spiritual – for the building of the Temple, speedily in our days.

The Elimination of the Mission
The elimination of the missionary plague from Israel by all means. The expropriation of the mission's property, and putting it at the disposal of needy Jews.

Less government
A free economy, in which private initiative, freed from the bonds of excessive government supervision, will invigorate the production lines. Correlating wages and productivity. The establishment of realistic taxation, in order to prevent tax evasion. The building of a Jewish economy based on Jewish manpower.

The Shield of the Entire People
Investing a supreme effort for the liberation of our brothers in Russia, Syria, Ethiopia, and other countries of distress. The State of Israel is the shield of all Jews wherever they live. The responsibility for their security rests solely on it. The issuing of a call for an emergency immigration from all the Diasporas, and especially from the United States, before a Holocaust descends upon them, G-d forbid.

A. B. C. [Atomic, Biological, and Chemical Warfare]
The planning and development of deterrent weaponry. The allocation of all the resources necessary for this.

The Removal of Traitors
The outlawing of Rakah [the Israeli Communist Party, currently named the Democratic Front for Peace and Equality], which is a fifth column.

Faith and Trust in G-d

A call to every Jew, wherever he is, to return to the path of the Torah and commandments, the path which maintained the existence of the people in the Exile, and which will maintain its existence in the future. The establishment of a complete Jewish state; total Sabbath observance; conversion in accordance with Jewish law; the cancellation of abortions; the cancellation of civil marriage; nonrecognition of Reform and Conservative Jews and their institutions. Faith and trust in G-d, the Stronghold and Redeemer of Israel.

"Thus," and only "thus" [a play on words; the Hebrew word *kach* means "thus"] will we bring closer the complete Redemption, speedily in our days.

Proposed law submitted by MK Rabbi Meir Kahane to Shlomo Hillel, speaker of the Eleventh Knesset. The Knesset Presidium (the Speaker and his deputies) decided on December 3, 1984 not to permit the bill to be entered on the Knesset calendar.

Proposed Law for the Prevention of Assimilation between Jews and Non-Jews and for the Sanctity of the Jewish People

I.   In an attempt to prevent assimilation, absorption, and intermarriage:

1.   All the programs of the Education Ministry and all other government ministries and bodies which are intended or are liable to lead to assimilation, absorption, and intermarriage shall be cancelled.

Inter alia, the following will be cancelled:

a.   mixed summer camps, community centers, and all mixed institutions.

b.   programs for visits by Jewish and Arab students to villages and homes.

c.   trips and visits abroad, in the course of which Jewish students are hosted in non-Jewish homes, as well as similar visits to Israel by non-Jews.

d.   mixed student dormitories in universities and colleges.

e.   permits for non-Jewish volunteers to work in kibbutzim or in other [forms of] volunteering.

2. All educational institutions in Eretz Israel, including day-care centers for preschool children, kindergartens, primary and secondary schools, institutions for higher learning and vocational training, and every other institution, will be separate for Jews and non-Jews.

3. Separate beaches, with no difference in their quality, will be established for Jews and non-Jews. A member of one people found on the beach intended for the members of the other people will be punished by imprisonment of one half year.

4. A non-Jew will not be permitted to live in a Jewish neighborhood without the consent of a majority of the Jewish residents of this building, or, in the case of a private house or a building with less than five residents, the consent of a majority of the Jews living in this area.

5. The Education Ministry will prepare curriculum for primary and secondary schools against assimilation, absorption, and intermarriage. This curriculum will emphasize the uniqueness of the Jewish People and the historical and traditional reasons for the opposition of the Jewish People throughout the ages to these phenomena. This curriculum will also emphasize the difference between separation, distinction, and seclusion and "racism." The Education Ministry will include in this curriculum a warning against the Christian mission and the Eastern cults, and will explain to the pupils the danger which they constitute for the Jewish People.

II. 1. Any institution or person belonging to any non-Jewish religion or cult or belief, who preaches or writes or gives speeches or lectures or teaches or attempts to persuade by any means, orally or in writing, by means of printed and stencilled material, or by means of films and broadcasts, including the various forms of the media, a Jew to convert or to accept, according to him, in addition to Judaism any religious principle which is opposed to Judaism, or who issues an invitation to, or publicizes among, the general public religious lessons or speeches or holds religious assemblies or meetings, the intent of which is to preach or teach the principles of a religion or belief other than Judaism, or who knows that Jews are within another religious framework, and does not remove them, his activity will be halted and he will be expelled from Israel.

2. A person born a Jew who commits the acts mentioned in section II(1) will be punished with five years' imprisonment.

3. An institution whose activity has been suspended and which was expelled from the country as a result of the actions mentioned in section II(1), and which returns disguised as another institution shall be punished by the confiscation of all its property.

4. A person who was expelled from the country for the actions mentioned in section II(1) and who returns shall be punished with three years' imprisonment and a deterrent fine, to be determined by the court.

III. 1. Jews and Jewesses, citizens and residents of the State, are forbidden to marry non-Jews, whether in Israel or abroad, in any form of religious or civil marriage.

IV. Such mixed marriages will not be recognized at all as marriages, even if they are recognized in the countries in which they were held, and the couple shall not enjoy any rights or benefits which the law imparts to married couples.

V. Jews and Jewesses, citizens of the State, are forbidden to have full or partial sexual relations of any sort with non-Jews, out of wedlock as well. The transgressor of this section shall be punished with two years' imprisonment.

VI. A non-Jew(ess) who seduces a Jew(ess) to marry him/her or to have any sort of sexual relations with him/her shall be punished with three years' imprisonment.

1. A non-Jew(ess) who impersonates a Jew(ess) and seduces a Jew(ess) to marry him/her or to have any sort of sexual relations with him/her shall be punished with five years' imprisonment.

2. A non-Jew who has sexual relations with a Jewish prostitute or with a Jewish male shall be punished with fifty years' imprisonment; a Jewish prostitute or Jewish male who has relations with a non-Jewish male shall be imprisoned with five years' imprisonment.

VII. The court will have no discretionary powers during the imposition of terms of imprisonment for the abovementioned crimes.

VIII. If the Jew(ess) did not know that his/her partner was a non-Jew(ess), the Jew(ess) may sue for monetary compensation for the mental distress which he/she caused, in adddition to the punishment of imprisonment established by this law.

IX. The partners in a mixed marriage which has already been performed will be compelled to separate immediately.

X. The children of the couple will, in all instances, remain in the custody of their mother, and their religious or national affiliation shall be that of their mother.

XI. Sections III through VII of this law are in force within the boundaries of the State of Israel and in all the territories under its control.

XII. The claim that the non-Jew did not know that his partner was a Jew(ess) does not constitute a defense, and does not exempt him/her from punishment under this law.

XIII. 1. Prostitution and procuring shall be transferred from the jurisdiction of the police to a special department in the Prime Minister's Office, with special investigators and Border Police subordinate to it.

2. The punishment for pimps shall be made more severe, and a person convicted of procuring shall be punished with life imprisonment.

3. The family of a non-Jewish pimp who is a resident of Eretz Israel shall be expelled from the State of Israel, and their possessions will be transferred to a special fund for the rehabilitation of Jewish prostitutes.

XIV. The punishment for alien residents who reside in the territories and who sleep within the boundaries of the State of Israel without a permit shall be made more severe, and they shall be punished with three years' imprisonment. An accomplice to this crime shall be punished with two years' imprisonment.

Explanatory Material

The plague of assimilation, absorption, and intermarriage has claimed and is claiming many victims within the Jewish People in the Diaspora, and there is hardly any house where there was not someone "dead" [Kahane makes extensive use of Biblical language and imagery; cf. Ex. 12:30 – trans.]. Jewish leaders in the Diaspora as well as in the State of Israel – including the President – have raised their voices against this cancer.

The plague has not passed over the Jewish State – the State of Israel – and, to our sorrow, a generation arose which did not know [cf. Ex. 1:8 – trans.] the sanctity and unity of the Jewish People, and which is willing to tear down the barriers between the sanctified and pure Jewish People and the other peoples of the world. Intermarriage, assimilation, and absorption are spreading in the State, and hardly anyone opens his mouth. Jewish tradition is clear: strong opposition to this plague, and, where possible, [taking] a strong hand against it.

"You shall be holy to Me, for I the Lord am holy, and I have set you apart from other peoples to be Mine" (Leviticus 20). Separation! Our holy Torah provides the tone, and the Jew – every Sabbath – repeats this when he lifts the cup of wine and proclaims, "Who has divided between sanctified and profane, between Israel and the nations!" Not a fusion, not a mixing, not integration – but rather a separation, as is fitting for a "holy nation" (Exodus 19), which is defined by the Sages in the *Mekhilta* (ibid.) as "holy and sanctified, separated from the peoples of the world and their abominations."

And the Torah commands about this: "You shall not intermarry with them: do not give your daughters to their sons or take their daughters for your sons" (Deuteronomy 7). Why? "Because you are a holy nation, and it is not proper that you shoud profane your holiness to beget invalid seed, as it is said (Malachi 2), "Judah has broken faith; abhorrent things have been done in Israel and in Jerusalem. For Judah has profaned

202

what is holy to the Lord – what He desires – and espoused daughters of alien gods" (*Seforno* on Deuteronomy 7).

When the Jewish People returned from the Babylonian Exile, when the Jews had the upper hand, the people's leaders took steps to prevent this phenomenon: "The people of Israel and the priests and Levites have not separated themselves from the peoples of the land ... They have taken their daughters as wives for themselves and their sons, so that the holy seed has become intermingled with the peoples of the land..." (Ezra 9). "Also at that time I saw that Jews had married Ashdodite, Ammonite, and Moabite women.... I censured them, cursed them, flogged them..." (Nehemiah).

Similarly, Maimonides rules: "If an Israelite has intercourse with a heathen woman of the other nations, by way of legal marriage.... they are liable to be flogged on the authority of the Torah.... If an Israelite has intercourse with a heathen woman by way of adultery, he is, on the authority of the Sages, liable only to the flogging prescribed for disobedience, which serves as a precaution, lest such intercourse should lead to intermarriage" (*Hil. Issurei Bi'ah* 12:1-2).

Being the Knesset of Israel, we are obligated to follow the path of the people's forefathers, to put an end to the spiritual holocaust in our midst, and to enact legislation which shall do this.

Proposed law submitted by MK Rabbi Meir Kahane to Shlomo Hillel, speaker of the Eleventh Knesset. The Knesset Presidium (the Speaker and his deputies) decided on December 3, 1984 not to permit the bill to be entered on the Knesset calendar.

Proposed Law for Israeli Citizenship and for Jewish and Arab Population Transfer

Definitions: In this law – "a member of the Jewish people" – whoever was born to a Jewish mother or who converted according to Jewish religious law.

"Jewish religious law" – every verse from the Bible or Rabbinic statement or ruling or law cited by legal authorities, including the commentary of one of the *Rishonim* [early authorities who preceded the writing of the *Shulhan Arukh*, the Code of Jewish Law)] or *Aharonim* [later authorities] who is accepted as a legal authority.

"Resident alien" – any non-Jew wishing to live in Eretz Israel and who accepts upon himself the seven Noachide Laws, i.e., the prohibition of idol worship, blasphemy, bloodshed, illicit sexual conduct, theft, and the eating of limbs from a still-living animal, as well as the commandment to maintain laws (courts which ensure a proper and just society).

"slavery" – "They are given inferior status, that they shall not lift up their heads in Israel, but rather be subjected to them, that they not be appointed to any office that will put them in charge of Israel" (Maimonides, *Hil. Melakhim* 6:1).

"taxes" – "that they be prepared to serve the king (the government) with their body and their money" (Maimonides, *Hil. Melakhim* 6:1).

I. Jewish law shall be used in order to determine the right of a non-Jew to live in Eretz Israel.

II. Only a member of the Jewish people may be a citizen of the State of Israel. A non-Jew may convert in accordance with the laws of the Torah.

III. A non-Jew who wishes to dwell in Eretz Israel, without distinction of religion, race, or nationality, will have to assume the Jewish legal status of "resident alien," and to declare this assumption in writing, by means of a sworn affidavit before a judge. In this document, every non-Jew shall also have to take, before a judge, an unreserved loyalty oath to the State of Israel as a Jewish state, and to the sovereignty of the Jewish People over its entire land.

IV. A special government commission, composed of qualified rabbis and experts on various religions, will be established to investigate the various religions and religious communities in Israel and to determine which of them are classified as idol worship.

V. The government shall determine the maximal number of resident aliens who may be settled in Eretz Israel without endangering the security of the State, and shall examine once per year whether this number has to be changed.

204

VI. Every "resident alien" will also assume the obligations of "taxes and slavery" as defined by Jewish religious law; if he will indeed do this, he will be permitted to live in Eretz Israel.

VII. 1. The personal and individual rights of a resident alien, without distinction of religion, race, or nationality, such as cultural, religious, social, and economic rights, shall be guaranteed, to the extent that they do not contradict Jewish religious law. Any Jewish citizen who shall express himself against a resident alien, or shall commit any act of discrimination against him, in contradiction to Jewish religious law, shall be placed on trial.

2. A resident alien may not live within the municipal boundaries of the city of Jerusalem.

3. A resident alien shall have no national rights nor shall he take any part in political proceedings in the State of Israel. A resident alien may not be appointed to any position of authority, and will not be able to vote in the elections to the Knesset or to any other state and public body, as defined by Jewish religious law (Deuteronomy 17:15; Babylonian Talmud, tractate Yevamot 45; Maimonides, *Hil. Melakhim* 1:4, 6:1).

4. Any violation by a "resident alien" of one of his obligations towards the seven Noachide Laws, taxes and slavery will bring in its wake immediate expulsion from Israel. A violation in other areas of any of the laws of the land will be considered, for the purposes of this law, as a deviation from the declaration of loyalty to the State, and is liable to lead to his expulsion.

VIII. Only Israeli citizens and "resident aliens" shall be permitted to live within the boundaries of the State of Israel and the territories under its control. A non-Jew who shall not agree to assume the halakhic [Jewish legal] status of "resident alien" (excluding non-Jews who serve here as representatives of foreign states or as representatives of the media from abroad or as various commercial representatives or tourists, up to one month) shall be removed from the country, either of his own free will, or against his will.

IX. In order to assist the non-Jew who willingly leaves Israel, the government shall establish information teams among Diaspora Jewry, in order to explain the problem of a hostile minority which is liable to become a majority within the State of Israel, and the important role of world Jewry in aiding the transferral of these people. Similarly, a fund will be established, with the assistance of world Jewry, to compensate those leaving for their property which shall be left in Israel. Special bonds will be issued for this purpose, similar to the Israel Bonds, and will be sold among world Jewry.

X. A commission shall be established which shall investigate and determine the exact sum of the compensation to each non-Jew who prefers to voluntarily leave Israel. A certain sum shall be deducted from each determination, which shall constitute a portion of the value of the property of the Jews of Arab countries who abandoned their property when they immigrated to Israel, for which they received no compensation. The sum which shall be deducted shall be placed in a special fund, and shall be distributed to Jews from Arab countries, as the commission shall determine.

XI. Every non-Jew who will not be willing to assume the status of resident alien and the obligations of taxes and slavery and who will not be willing to voluntarily leave Israel, shall be forcibly removed from here.

XII. Until the abovementioned measures shall be adopted:

1. The National Insurance Institute shall be transferred from the government to the Jewish Agency, so that only Jews will be able to benefit from its payments.

2. Every non-Jew will be required at the age of 18 to engage for three years in non-military National Service, in construction works, etc. Non-Jews will also have reserves duty, the format of which shall be identical to the military reserves duty which is incumbent upon Jews.

3. The exact location of all non-Jewish houses which have

206

been built without a permit since the establishment of the State until the present will be determined. These houses shall be immediately razed.

4. A special branch shall be established in the Income Tax Commission whose task shall be to supervise and collect from non-Jews the taxes which they are required to pay, as well as to examine the issue of tax evasion.

XIII. A special government Ministry for Emigration shall be established, which shall be responsible for the implementation of the sections of this law. Special offices will be established within this Ministry to register non-Jews who will be willing to emigrate, and shall inform them of their rights and responsibilities under the law.

Explanatory Material

The flight of Jews from Arab and Moslem lands, accompanied by a violent expulsion with no compensation for confiscated property, began with the establishment of the Jewish State in 5708 [1948]. In the end, more than seven hundred thousand Jews came from Arab and Moslem countries to the State of Israel, with less than eighty thousand left today in the Arab countries.

At the same time, about five hundred thousand Arabs fled from the State of Israel, leaving about one hundred and fifty thousand after the establishment of the State. Since then, despite the continual immigration of Jews to the State, the percentage of the Arab population within the State of Israel (i.e., in the territory of Eretz Israel exclusive of Judea, Samaria, Gaza, or the Golan) has gradually risen, until it now stands at close to 18 percent of the general population. This impressive increase has been built almost exclusively on birth, natural increase without an addition of Arabs from the outside.

The Arab birthrate in Israel continues to be astounding, more than twice the Jewish birthrate; when one considers the facts of a low Jewish birthrate, a sorry immigration of Jews from the Diaspora, and migration from the country which is more than the immigration to it, it can be understood that the Arab population is gradually arriving at percentages which endanger the wellbeing of the Jewish-Zionist state, and will eventually endanger its very existence as a Jewish-Zionist state. This will occur when the Arabs become an absolute majority, and will under no circumstances agree to live in a "Jewish" state when they are the majority.

Political Zionism came into being in order to establish a Jewish, sovereign, and free state for the Jewish People, and indeed, the Declaration of Independence so proclaims: "We hereby declare the establishment of a Jewish state in Eretz-Israel...." There is no possibility of establishing such a state unless the Jews within it are the majority of the population. The great illusion that it is possible to persuade the Arabs to agree to be peaceful citizens within the Jewish state, whose entire spirit is Jewish, and whose anthem speaks of a "Jewish soul," and which has close ties with world Jewry, is only a demonstration of contempt for and debasement of the Arabs. The Arab will not agree to accept the Jewish state in return for a rise in his economic standard of living or for education. For the Arab man does not live by bread alone. He demands a state of his own, and dreams of the day when he will be the majority here, and democracy and peace will transform "Israel" into "Palestine."

In the light of all this, and in light of the fact that sizeable portions of the State, such as the Galilee, Wadi Ara and the Triangle, already have an Arab majority, we propose a law which will protect the Jews of the State of Israel and which will lead to the second stage of the population transfer which began in 5708 [1948], with the exodus of the Jews from the Arab lands. It is also important to note that this law in practice fulfills the Hebrew law, i.e., the Jewish religious law, as it defines the status of the non-Jew in Eretz Israel.

In preparation for the Knesset discussion on limiting Meir Kahane's parliamentary immunity, Likud MK Michael Eitan analyzed Kahane's "shocking" proposed laws, comparing them with two Nazi laws enacted on September 15, 1935 (the "Nuremburg laws"), the "Reich Citizenship Law" and the "Law for the Protection of German Blood and Honor." These two laws served as the basis for the entire stucture of Nazi racial legislation. Eitan, a diehard member of the "national camp," was stunned by the similarities between the two sets of laws, and prepared the following chart:

Kahane's proposals

Status of Non-Jews
1. Without any national rights, and without any part in political proceedings in the State of Israel. May not be appointed to any position of authority, and will not be able to vote in the elections to the Knesset or to any other state and public body.
2. Will assume the obligations of taxes and slavery. If he will not agree to taxes and slavery, he will forcibly be expelled.

Restrictions on Residence
A non-Jew may not live within the municipal boundaries of the city of Jerusalem.

Prohibition of Intermarriage
Jews and Jewesses, citizens and residents of the State, are forbidden to marry non-Jews, whether in Israel or abroad ... Such mixed marriages will not be recognized at all as marriages.

Extramarital Relations
1. Jews and Jewesses, citizens of the State, are forbidden to have full or partial sexual relations of any sort with non-Jews, out of wedlock as well. The transgressor of this section shall be punished with two years' imprisonment.
2. A non-Jew who has sexual relations with a Jewish prostitute or with a Jewish male shall be punished with fifty years' imprisonment; a Jewish prostitute or Jewish male who has relations with a non-Jewish male shall be punished with five years' imprisonment.

Separation of Students
All educational institutions in Eretz Israel will be separate for Jews and non-Jews.

Prevention of Meetings between Youth
Mixed summer camps, community centers, and all mixed institutions will be cancelled. Programs for visits by Jewish and Arab pupils to villages and homes will be cancelled. Trips and visits abroad, in the course of which Jewish pupils are hosted in non-Jewish homes, as well as similar visits to Israel by non-Jews, will be cancelled.

Separate Beaches
Separate beaches, with no difference in their quality, will be established for Jews and non-Jews. A member of one people found on the beach intended for the members of the other people will be punished by imprisonment of one half year.

Nazi legislation

Status of Jews
Jews cannot be citizens of the Reich. They have no right to vote politically, and cannot hold public office.
November 14, 1935: First Regulation to the Reich Citizenship Law.

Restrictions on Residence
Apartments in Berlin and Munich which had been rented to Jews will not be rented again to a Jew, to his wife, or to a Jewish enterprise without a special permit.
Regulation of the Reich Labor Minister. February 8, 1939.

Prohibition of Intermarriage
Marriages between Jews and citizens of the state of German blood, or of blood close to it, are forbidden. Marriages which were conducted illegally are cancelled, even if they were conducted abroad.

Section 1 of the Law for the Protection of German Blood and Honor, September 15, 1939.

Extramarital Relations between Jews and Citizens of the Reich
1. Extramarital relations between Jews and subjects of the state of German blood, or blood close to it, are forbidden. Section 2 of the Law for the Protection of German Blood and Honor.
2. Jews are not permitted to employ for housework subjects of the state of German blood, or of blood close to it, who are under the age of 45.
Section 3 of the Law for the Protection of German Blood and Honor.

Separation of Students
It is forbidden for Jewish students to study in German schools. They are permitted to study only in Jewish schools.
Regulation of the Nazi Minister of Education, November 15, 1938.

Prevention of Meetings between Youth
1. It is forbidden to include non-Aryan boy and girl pupils in a visit to youth hostels.
Regulation of the Bavarian Minister of Education, July 31, 1935.
2. It is intolerable that Jewish pupils will participate in school activities in which they are liable to come into physical contact with German pupils.
Regulation of the Baden Minister of Education, November 3, 1938.

Separation in Swimming Pools and in Resorts
1. It is forbidden for Jews to enter public swimming pools.
August 1935, regulations of various local authorities.
2. Jews and non-Jews must be separated in resorts and health resorts. Accordingly, Jews must be accomodated in separate hotels and pensions. In resorts and health resorts where there are facilities for the shared use of many, Jews and non-

Jews must be separated. If separation is not possible, Jews will be forbidden entry.
Reich Interior Minister, July 24, 1937.